THE BOW-WOW CLUB

A Play in Two Acts
by
LEVY "LEE" SIMON JR.

Dramatic Publishing
Woodstock, Illinois • England • Australia • New Zealand

IMPORTANT BILLING AND CREDIT REQUIREMENTS

All producers of the play *must* give credit to the author(s) of the play in all programs distributed in connection with performances of the play and in all instances in which the title of the play appears for purposes of advertising, publicizing or otherwise exploiting the play and/or a production. The name of the author(s) *must* also appear on a separate line, on which no other name appears, immediately following the title, and *must* appear in size of type not less than fifty percent the size of the title type. Biographical information on the author(s), if included in this book, may be used on all programs. *On all programs this notice must appear:*

"Produced by special arrangement with
THE DRAMATIC PUBLISHING COMPANY of Woodstock, Illinois"

For all those who have gone before the rest of us when it seemed just a little too early. Thank you for sharing and giving us laughter and tears. For all all the parents, who did the best they could. And for all of us still trying to make sense of the journey.

THE BOW-WOW CLUB was first performed at the University of Iowa (Gallery Production), October 1997. Edris Cooper directed the production, which included the following cast:

Diane	SHERRI MARINA
Kirk	ELGIN BURNETTE
Sal	LANRE IDEWU
Bev	NICOLE BUTLER
Alex	LAWRENCE THOMAS
Freida	BARI NEWPORT
Chuck	ANSA AKYEA
Lester	DOUGLAS HOWINGTON
Loita	EMILY DRACH
Perry	MARC BURG

The Iowa Playwrights Festival cast (May 1998)

Diane	SHERRI MARINA
Kirk	ELGIN BURNETTE
Sal	BILL CAISE
Bev	KAMI WILLIAMS
Alex	ANSA AKYEA
Freida	MOLLY ARMOUR
Chuck	CECIL SLAUGHTER
Lester	DOUGLAS HOWINGTON
Loita	EMILY DRACH
Perry	MARC BURG
Sal (alternate performer)	LEE SIMON, JR.

AUTHOR'S NOTE

The Bow-Wow Club is a serious comedy about friendship, love, responsibility, and survival. Though the subject matter is serious, directors and actors should not avoid the humor in the play. In fact, the humor should be exploited as often as situations and lines suggest.

THE BOW-WOW CLUB

A Play in Two Acts
For 6 Men and 4 Women

CHARACTERS
(in order of appearance)

DIANE BRIGHT . . . . late 30s, married to Kirk

KIRK BRIGHT. . . . . . late 30s, early retiree from the army

SAL ANDERSON . . . . transit worker

BEVERLY ANDERSON . . . . married to Sal

ALEXANDER EARLE . . . . . . late 30s, a college professor

FREIDA EARLE . 35, a college professor, married to Alex

CHUCK HOOTER . . . . late 30s, associate professor

LESTER MCMICHEAL . . . . . . late 30s, singer and dancer

LOITA CLARVEAX . . . . 25, French model

PERRY PENNICK . . . . early 30s

SETTING
Act One: Diane and Kirk's home in Maryland.
Act Two: A park in Maryland.

ACT ONE

SCENE ONE

AT RISE: *Lights come up on DIANE in the kitchen. She is preparing potato salad. There are pots on the stove. One should get the feeling that this is her domain. She is comfortable in the kitchen and has no problem being there. KIRK enters the house from the archway, carrying two large shopping bags.*

KIRK. Dee! Dee! Hey, Dee! Dee!

DIANE. I'm in the kitchen, Kirk. You don't have to do all that screaming.

(KIRK enters the kitchen with shopping bags.)

KIRK. Any calls?

DIANE. No.

KIRK. Sal said he was gonna call when they got through Delaware. They should have been through Delaware already.

DIANE. Kirk, you are not in the army anymore. You can't keep everybody on a schedule. All that crying you did about getting out of the military, and look at you. Relax, we are civilians now.

KIRK. As always, you are right, Boobbie—Boobbie. God, I
can't believe it. Do you know the last time the Bow-
Wow Club was all together, the five of us?

DIANE. Almost twenty years, Kirk. I know.

KIRK. Yep. Over twenty years. *(Opens bag.)* Look what I
got. *(He takes some items from the shopping bag.)*

DIANE *(not looking)*. I know what you got, Kirk.

KIRK. Well, just humor me then.

DIANE. I ain't got time to humor you. I'm trying to cook
some of this food now. So I won't have to cook all day
tomorrow. And if I don't cook it now they won't be any
food tomorrow unless you cook it yourself, because I
ain't cooking tomorrow. Not gonna have me cooking on
the Fourth of July while y'all sit around having all the
fun.

KIRK. I already told you, me and Sal gonna do all the barbecuing. Ribs, burgers, chicken, hot dogs. Ruff-ruff.
Come on Dee, humor me.

DIANE *(holding a spoon)*. I got your humor.

KIRK *(pulling each item from the bag)*. Colt .45 for Sal.
Chivas Regal for Alex.

DIANE. I thought he stopped drinking.

KIRK. Yeah, but this is the Bow-Wow reunion.

DIANE. Humph.

KIRK. In case he didn't, this is what he used to drink.
Remy Martin, for Lester, and Chocolate Yoo-hoo for
Chuck. I bet you don't know who gets the Colt .45.

DIANE. You just said Sal!

KIRK. That's right, Sal. Man-o-man, we usta do our football workout in the summertime from ten in the morning
to four in the afternoon. We take a break and then we

work out from six to eight at night. We wasn't bulljiving!

DIANE. That's why y'all are crazy now, running in all that hot sun, damaged your brains.

KIRK. You got that right. After that, I go get my old E., and Sal get his Colt .45, and we was good to go. And on Fridays—

DIANE & KIRK. We go get a big bag of Scottie's nickel bag of reefer with twenty-one joints.

DIANE. Kirk, you told me these stories a thousand times, and it ain't like I wasn't there. Me and Bev, we know the stories better than y'all.

(As KIRK puts the items away he pops open a can of Old English.)

KIRK. Dee, you know something?

DIANE. What, Kirk?

KIRK. You look as good as you did twenty years ago.

DIANE. Yeah, after three kids and thirty pounds.

KIRK. Yep. After three kids and thirty-five pounds.

DIANE. I'm gonna hit you with this pot. You gained a few yourself, mister, talking about me. *(He holds her.)* Stop, Kirk, I'm trying to cook.

KIRK. But you still got them dimples. That's when I knew I was gonna love you forever. When I saw them dimples on your butt, I said to myself, she can get skinny, or she can stay fat, but them dimples ain't going nowhere. *(He touches her behind.)*

DIANE. Come on, Kirk, leave my dimples alone. Let me go so I can make this potato salad before your friends get here.

KIRK. Dee, let's get busy first.

DIANE. Busy? I got your busy. *(He continues to feel on DIANE.)* No, Kirk. *(He stops for a moment.)*

KIRK. Damn! The Bow-Wow Club back together.

DIANE. What I told you about cursing in the house. See, that's why you so hot and bothered, thinking about when you was seventeen, but face it, Kirk, you ain't seventeen no more.

KIRK. You got that right. Now I got experience. I'm like good wine.

DIANE. I ain't no wine drinker so I wouldn't know.

KIRK. Like the young bull and the old bull—

DIANE. And I told you about that old nasty bull joke. Don't nobody want to hear that in here this evening.

KIRK. You know what I'm talking about. Staying power. *(He begins to unzip her.)*

DIANE. You wanna cook this food?

KIRK. Dee, you know I love the fellas. I don't want to kill them with my cooking!

DIANE. Leave me alone then.

KIRK *(takes a sip of beer)*. Good googa mooga. Lester flying in from France!

DIANE. I thought he was in Canada.

KIRK. That was last week. He opened a concert in Paris two nights ago, I think.

DIANE. That man. He bringing that woman he was in the magazine with, that French model?

KIRK. Knowing Lester, he might come here with a whole bevy of bitc— I mean babes, women. My man Lester. Bow-Wow to the core.

DIANE. He needs to settle down. Even dogs don't stay in heat all the time.

KIRK. Not Lester. If Lester ever settled down it would be headline news. They call Bryant Gumble back to *The Today Show* for that one.

DIANE. He might catch something he won't get rid of. Put my dress back on, Kirk!

KIRK. Ruff, ruff.

DIANE. All right now, don't get carried away. The only reason I'm putting up with this is because I know you drive me crazy if I said no.

KIRK. Shoot, you know you want to see everybody just as bad as I do. I ever tell you how—

DIANE. Yes, Kirk.

KIRK. Be good for you to see Bev.

DIANE. Next time I'm sending you on vacation, and me and Bev gonna have a Me-ow Club reunion.

KIRK. Ruff, ruff.

DIANE. Old dog.

KIRK. Pedigree though. Don't forget that. From the dog pound of Harlem, U.S.A. Ruff—ruff—ruff. *(KIRK stalks then chases DIANE around the kitchen. He finally corners her. She raises a pot.)*

DIANE. Get away from me! *(KIRK backs away from her, a bit dejected.)* Chuck tell you who he bringing?

KIRK. Naw. I can't believe Chuck been living right in D.C. for the last three years.

DIANE. That is a shame, though. All these years and y'all ain't talked.

KIRK. It ain't my fault. You know me, I'm gonna keep in contact with everybody. I wonder if he look like a preacher.

DIANE. A minister. And because he was a minister ain't gonna make him look no different. I don't know how he thought he was gonna be a minister and couldn't keep the commandments. Up in the church committing adultery.

KIRK. That's why I called him a preacher. Everybody knows the preacher be checking out the dames in the first row, with they hats on and legs crossed, talking about Amen. They probably heard him scream Amen! the night before. I can hear him now. Amen! Amen! Lord have mercy!

DIANE. Kirk, you about to make me send you to the garage. You getting beside yourself.

KIRK. I'm just making a point. Ministers don't do that. But the preacher—

DIANE. Shut up, Kirk, you crazy.

KIRK. I just wonder if he changed.

DIANE. Kirk! You changed! They all changed. Don't you go getting all disappointed when you find that out. All I need this weekend is for you to start pouting.

KIRK. I ain't gonna be pouting. Sal ain't changed. Lester a star, and he ain't changed. Alex the only one shocked everybody with his white woman.

DIANE. Lester be with them white women too now.

KIRK. Yeah, but that's different, Lester's a star. But, Alex Felix Earle, the most militant one of us, goes and marries a white dame.

DIANE. Maybe he loves her, Kirk.

KIRK. Yeah, well, I am dying to find out. He can have his turkey breast, give me the drumstick every time. *(He pulls her dress off.)*

DIANE. I'm gonna burn you with these potatoes.

KIRK. Whoo. Just make me hotter, snookum-wookum!

DIANE. Kirk!

(He kisses her neck and body.)

KIRK. Who woulda thunk it. As much as I loved you twenty years ago that I could love you even more.

DIANE. I know I ain't gonna get my work done until I give you some. OK. You asked for it. You ready. Getting me all hot and bothered.

KIRK. My middle name is Teddy and I want you to meet Freddy. *(They begin to kiss passionately. KIRK has stripped DIANE to her slip. She strips his pants. They are passionate. The doorbell rings.)* Shit-shoot!

DIANE *(rising and straightening up)*. See, I knew I should have followed my own mind. *(KIRK goes to the door.)* Kirk, wait!

(KIRK waits a second, then opens the door. SAL enters. KIRK extends a greeting. SAL walks by him. He ignores DIANE getting dressed.)

SAL. What's up, Kirk? Bev, would you come on, shit.

(BEVERLY enters. She sits at the kitchen table.)

SAL. Yo, man, let me tell you something. I'm driving, right?

BEV. OK, listen to this.

SAL. I'm talking here.

BEV. Go ahead, talk then!

SAL. The sign says Silver Springs exit 32, right?

BEV. Dee, didn't you say get off at exit 34?

SAL. The sign said Silver Spring exit 32. Where do y'all live, Silver Spring, right?

BEV. I took the directions from Dee.

SAL. I don't care if you took directions from the mailman. You always got to question everything I do.

BEV. Well, I have a mind too, excuse me.

SAL. That's the problem. You think you smarter than everybody else, got all the answers. *(He opens a can of Colt .45 without looking.)*

BEV. The problem is, you don't want to listen. He's speeding down the highway like he knows where he going.

SAL. Ever since she been in that damn law school she think she can talk to me any way she wants to. Well, I got a Sue Simmons *Live at Five* news flash for you, baby.

BEV. Law school don't have nothing to do with it. I wasn't paying attention to you long before I went to law school. So what you really need to do is get over it. Hi, Dee.

DIANE. Hey, Bev.

BEV. This is a beautiful house.

SAL. You see that shit. I wasn't finish talking.

BEV. Show me the house, Dee.

DIANE. I'm gonna show Bev the house, Kirk. *(They exit.)*

SAL. That woman gets on my last nerve. Like a migraine toothache.

KIRK. So how you doing, Sal, ohh buddy, oh pal.

SAL. You see how I'm doing. Dealing with the wicked witch of the east. *(Really sees KIRK for the first time.)* Oh shit. Kirk! Damn, man!

KIRK. Sal-onse! *(They hug.)*

SAL. Damn, you look good, man. Where's Justice, and Jasper, and my little cutie-pie, Jasmine?

KIRK. I told you on the invite man, no kids. Justice and Jasper at football camp and Jasmine is with Dee's mom.

We gonna parta this weekend. Hey, Sal, guess what I got? *(Pulls a bottle of Myers' rum from the bag.)*

SAL. Good old Myers, hook it up, man.

KIRK. You still use lemon, lime, and cranberry juice? *(Gets items from the cupboard.)*

SAL. Forget that, on the rocks. Nice house.

KIRK. Finally.

SAL. When the fellas gonna get here?

KIRK. Alex suppose to be here tonight sometime. Chuck and Lester be here in the morning. Soon as they get here we are going to drive up to the lake, celebrate the Fourth up there. *(Firecrackers go off in the background.)*

SAL. Wow! Fourth of July at Kirk's house.

KIRK. You got that right. It ain't my dream house but it's a house. We got a lot more to do with it. These contractors try to get you at every angle, but later for that, the fellas all gonna be together, again.

SAL. Yep. Lester a damn star. Can you believe that shit?

KIRK. Soul Train Award-winner.

SAL. He sent me an invitation. I shoulda went but you know transit won't give me time off. I see why my pops usta call it a slave back in the day.

KIRK. You should have been there though. He had a babe badder than Paula Abdul!

SAL. I like that little Toni Braxton myself.

KIRK. You see him with the supermodel in Ebony.

SAL. Big deal. Shit, I remember when he couldn't buy pussy.

KIRK. You wrong there. All of us could get some pussy. That's why we formed the Bow-Wow Club. I got to admit, you was the man though. The original, "have dick will travel."

SAL. Yep, that was me, wasn't it?

KIRK. I never knew anybody to do seven women in one day.

SAL. Damn. Seven?

KIRK. Margaret, Venessa, Linda, Carmen. Adele, Evette, and April.

SAL. Damn, I don't even remember their names.

KIRK. Shoot, I remember Venessa usta have a bootie so big, it used to clap when the wind blew.

SAL. Bring back memories, boy! I woulda broke my own record if I didn't bust these knees and commit myself to eternal misery with Hella the Terrible.

KIRK. I still can't get over that. Your knees, I mean—

SAL. No use crying. That was a long time ago. Remember how we usta get that feeling in the pit of our stomach every fall. Cool air, leaves turning brown, sundown at five o'clock. I don't think about it anymore though. It's good to see you, man. You was the only one to show up for my son's funeral.

KIRK. Yeah. People get busy, Sal.

SAL. Yeah, I know. You was in Japan then, right?

KIRK. Yep.

SAL. I was so bummed out, I don't remember.

KIRK. Hey, I got a football in the garage. And I still got my Dewitt Clinton football jersey. I got two, as a matter of fact.

SAL. I'd die before I put a Dewitt Clinton jersey on. Blue and white. Richman Rams all the way.

KIRK. We usta bust y'all's ass! Oops, better not let Dee hear me cursing. She done got religion in her old age. Anyway, we go out tomorrow and throw a few.

SAL. Kirk, I don't even watch football anymore, man. Fuck football.

KIRK *(strikes a football pose)*. Hut one hut two.

SAL. My football days are over, Kirk. Why don't you sit down with yo old weekend warrior ass. *(Long pause. KIRK is unsure how to respond.)* Kirk, uh, you know Ollie Colvin still coaching.

KIRK. What!

SAL. Yeah, Julius was gonna start—

(He stops and takes a sip of his drink. The WOMEN re-enter.)

BEV. Sal, you should see the house.

SAL. What's that suppose to mean?

BEV. It means it's a nice house and you should see it.

SAL. I'm here. I got eyes. I'm gonna be here for the next three days. You don't think I'm gonna see the house. That's why we came, right, to see Kirk and Dee's new house. That is why we came, right?

BEV. I'll get the things out of the car.

SAL. No, I'll get the things out of the car. *(He starts to leave.)*

KIRK. Let me help you, Sal. I'll show you my part of the house. The garage. *(They exit.)*

BEV. Drives me crazy. I'm so tired of that man, Dee. I'm sorry, you invited us to enjoy your new house, and we come in here fighting like a cat and a dog. I'm going to try my best not to let him get to me, but that man—I'll get on a bus back to New York before I let us ruin your Fourth of July weekend.

DIANE. You better not go back, and leave me here with them. I love each one of them, but I don't know if I could take them all at once by myself. They drove me crazy when I was younger and I got a feeling when they get together it's going to be worse.

BEV *(short pause)*. It's been pretty bad, Dee.

DIANE. He's been through a lot, Bev.

BEV. And I haven't? Everybody thinks he's the only one who hurts. I don't understand that. We lost our only child. The two of us. Not him, not me, we. Julius was our son. Not just his.

DIANE. I know.

BEV. Well I wish someone would make him know that. I know he's had it bad, but I've had my share too.

DIANE. I know, Bev—

BEV. After "Officer Florintino" murdered Julius, I thought Sal was going to lose his mind, and it was half gone already. I was thinking about leaving him before that, but I couldn't leave him in the condition he was in. I wouldn't have been able to live with myself. Dee, we suppose to be having a good time, and I'm going on and on about my problems.

DIANE. Who's standing in front of you?

BEV. You.

DIANE. Well, all right then.

BEV. Aw, Dee. *(They hug.)* I can't wait to see that crazy behind Lester, and Alex.

DIANE. Didn't you meet this Freida woman?

BEV. I met her when they were in New York last year. She's nice enough. You know Alex, he always wants people to be at his beck and call, and she is at his beck and call.

(SAL and KIRK enter with bags.)

SAL. You think we was moving in. I told her we didn't need all this stuff.

KIRK. Hey, it's better to have too much than too little, huh?

BEV. I told him that.

SAL. My mother died over ten years ago?

BEV. Your mother ain't got nothing to do with this.

SAL. Well stop acting like you my mother then.

BEV. You need somebody to tell you something.

SAL. Here, you want my pants?

(SAL undoes his belt. ALEXANDER enters the back door with FREIDA who is three months pregnant.)

ALEX. Have no fear, Alexander the great is here! *(Long pause.)*

KIRK. What's up, Alex?

ALEX. Should we go out and come back in?

SAL. Naw, man. Alex, we just dealing with the fact that I married a woman who wants to wear my pants, that's all.

BEV. Somebody has got to wear them.

SAL. Lester told me not to marry you. He told me way back when, all you wanted to do was to grow one bigger than mine.

BEV. If you shared yours, I wouldn't have to grow my own.

SAL. You can't settle for sharing, you want the whole damn thing!

KIRK. All right! That's enough! Attention! I said attention! What's wrong with y'all. I invited the Bow-Wow Club to my house for a Fourth of July reunion. I didn't invite nobody to my house for a damn war. I'm out of the military. I am retired! I'm gonna tell y'all now I ain't gonna have all this fighting in my house. Sal, you my boy and always will be, and, Bev, I la' ya like a sister, but y'all gonna have to eighty-six the dumb shit. Now we are going to have a good time this weekend even if it kills everybody! Understand? I didn't hear y'all! Do you understand?

BEV. Yes—

KIRK. Sal.

SAL. I heard you, man.

KIRK. Alex?

ALEX. What?

KIRK. Understand?

ALEX. Yeah.

KIRK. What's your name again?

FREIDA. Freida.

KIRK. You understand?

ALEX. Just say yes.

FREIDA. Peace and love, man.

KIRK. I still got my weapon. For those of you who don't know what that is, I still got my .45. Come in my new house with this dumb shit. *(He exits. DIANE follows KIRK out. BEV follows DIANE. SAL exits through the kitchen door.)*

ALEX. Now you see why I didn't want to come.

FREIDA. Well you didn't tell me the dogs bite.

ALEX. All dogs bite, Freida, you know that.

(Lights fade.)

SCENE TWO

AT RISE: *Early morning, the next day. Fourth of July. DI-ANE is in the kitchen preparing breakfast. Coffee, doughnuts, rolls, etc. She hums a spiritual. Then speaks to herself.*

DIANE. Lord, thank you for all your blessings and please look over us this Fourth of July weekend. Give me the strength to persevere. And, Lord, don't let these boys get too crazy in—

(ALEX and FREIDA enter. ALEX is dressed in African print pj's. FREIDA is dressed in jeans and a T-shirt. Her hair is wet from the shower.)

ALEX. When'd you start talking to yourself, Dee?

DIANE. Just praising the Lord. How are you two this morning?

FREIDA. Fine.

DIANE. And how's the little cookie in the oven.

FREIDA. The little cookie in the oven is turning into a three-layer cake fast.

DIANE. You don't have to tell me. One minute you can see your feet and the next minute you can't. After Jasmine, I didn't know if I would ever see my feet again. First one?

FREIDA. First one.

DIANE. Old folks always say the first one is the hardest, but I don't know, that little Jasmine was something else. Forty-seven hours to convince her to come out.

FREIDA. Forty-seven hours!

DIANE. Only took Justice nineteen, but when they come out and you see those little hands and those little feet, it's worth every minute until they start getting they little minds of their own, then you start wondering, Lord, what was I thinking about.

FREIDA. Forty-seven hours. I can't imagine. No wonder I waited so long. Forty se—

ALEX. Glad it isn't me.

(FREIDA hits ALEX.)

DIANE. Listen to you. You need to go back to bed and wake up again.

ALEX. I could use some more sleep, I'll tell you that.

DIANE. You didn't sleep well last night?

ALEX. Between Sal and Bev arguing and Freida snoring I got maybe twenty minutes.

FREIDA. I wasn't snoring.

ALEX. As soon as your head hit the pillow, urrrrgh.

FREIDA. Alex Earle, stop that.

ALEX. It's true.

DIANE. Kirk went in there to talk to Sal three times last night but they be quiet for a while and then it start up, all over again.

FREIDA. I take it you didn't get much sleep either.

DIANE. No. They finally stopped around three this morning, then Chuck rang the bell.

ALEX. That nut they call Chuck is here? I can't remember the last time I saw Chuck Hooter.

DIANE. I'm mad at Chuck. You know he's been living right in D.C. for the past six years. Kirk went through all kinds of trouble trying to find him. He could have called us. Because we been here. I don't know what gets into people. He looks good though.

FREIDA. Chuck is the minister?

DIANE. Was?

ALEX. I'm glad he gave up that cloth, selling people a dream—

FREIDA. Alex.

DIANE. Ain't nothing wrong with the cloth. People don't know how to respect it. I am not passing any judgment on anybody, because everybody is going to have to answer to the Lord. I just mine my business, I ain't trying to be nobody's holy roller and I don't want any nonbelievers trying to stop me from praising the Lord. What y'all want for breakfast? Kirk went out last night and bought some bacon, pork sausages links, pancake mix, he got that hot kind of sausage, too. The kind they make down south with all the red pepper in it.

ALEX. We don't eat meat, Dee.

DIANE. Y'all don't eat no meat?

ALEX & FREIDA. No.

DIANE. Well I'll just whip you up some eggs.

ALEX. Dee. Freida's on a non-dairy vegetarian diet.

DIANE. No meat. No eggs.

FREIDA. I went to the farmers' market before I left and made sure to get everything we needed for the trip: bean sprouts, soy, three-grain bread, everything. Then we were rushing to get out of the house before rush-hour traffic and Alex left the bag right on the kitchen table.

DIANE. That's all you eat is bean sprouts and bread?

FREIDA. Some fish every now and then.

ALEX. Raw fish.

DIANE. You eat raw fish?

FREIDA. Some salmon every now and then. It's not as bad as it sounds.

DIANE. What about the baby? You better eat so that baby will be healthy. Your first time too.

ALEX. Freida thinks eating a macrobiotic diet is healthier.

DIANE. Healthier? If you say so.

ALEX. Raw fish, that's where I draw the line.

FREIDA. Alex, you know if I fix some sushi you'll gobble it up like Orca the whale.

ALEX. That's different, baby— *(They kiss.)*

DIANE *(to herself)*. Raw fish, hmm. *(To FREIDA.)* What about some cereal? I got frosted flakes.

FREIDA. I don't eat white sugar.

DIANE. Lord! Poor child.

FREIDA. Dee, it's fine. I'm used to it.

ALEX. If you weren't arguing with me when we left the house—

FREIDA. You wouldn't have forgot the food.

DIANE. What's everybody arguing about?

(FREIDA kisses ALEX passionately.)

DIANE. Now, see that's nice.

ALEX. I just wondered why Kirk had to have the reunion on the Fourth of July. Why couldn't you have it on the fifth of July, or the fourth of August. I don't celebrate these American holidays. The Fourth of July, black people still aren't free. Who's it for anyway? The big corporations? Hollywood? An excuse so they can put more movies out? *Men in Black*, *Aliens*, Harrison Ford. It's not for black people. Give me my forty acres and a mule, then I might celebrate Independence Day.

FREIDA. Alex, don't start.

DIANE. I don't believe Kirk thought about any of that. He just wanted to see the Bow-Wow Club back together.

FREIDA. It's nice that you all are getting together. The only time my family gets together is for someone's funeral. Family comes from all over the country, and they talk about how much they miss each other, and then the conversation always ends with how we should get together more. As soon as it's over, everybody goes home and no one even calls anybody until the next person dies.

ALEX. Freida just lost her stepdad about a month ago.

DIANE. I'm sorry to hear that.

FREIDA. Thank you. That's why I think it's important. You never know. I can't even remember the people I went to college or high school with.

ALEX. I don't think they want to remember you either.

FREIDA. Alex. I grew up in a little town in Georgia, very close to Forsythe County. My family. My grandmother still uses a rotary phone, and my mother thinks E-mail is a letter addressed to somebody named E. I won't even mention how they feel about Alex.

ALEX. Or how I feel about them.

DIANE. This is 1997. Pay them no mind.

ALEX. It could be 2097, racism isn't going anywhere. When I think—

FREIDA. Alex— *(She kisses ALEX again.)*

DIANE. That's nice— Sal and Bev should be here now.

ALEX. Is anybody sick or anything? Usually these kind of gatherings means there's some kind of big announcement coming.

DIANE. Any news you get will be news to me too.

ALEX. Good. The last thing I need is somebody saying they ready to kick the bucket or something.

FREIDA. Alex, why are you so morbid this morning?

ALEX. I'm not morbid. Dee, you think I'm morbid?

DIANE. No, you just like you always was, Alex, see the bright side of everything.

FREIDA. I want to hear all about the Bow-Wow Club. When Alex first told me about this infamous little club, I couldn't imagine what he was talking about.

DIANE. Child, nobody can imagine how these clowns were.

ALEX. Personally I feel we should leave the past in the past.

FREIDA. Listen to yourself. Mr. Forty Acres.

ALEX. She keeps me on my toes, Dee. That's why I love her. *(He kisses her.)*

DIANE. What are you going to feed that baby?

FREIDA. Any health food stores close by?

DIANE. Any what?

FREIDA. Health food stores?

DIANE. The A&P, that's about as healthy as it gets for me. Kirk might—never mind.

ALEX. We'll go out later and find one.

DIANE. The only thing I need to do is stop eating all these doughnuts. I'm just as fat.

ALEX. You look great, Dee.

(CHUCK enters. He is a neatly dressed man.)

CHUCK. You do look great, Dee. And speaking of looking great.

ALEX. The nut they call Chuck. It has been a long time. *(The two men hug.)*

CHUCK. Wow, look at you. If I saw you on the street, I wouldn't have known you.

ALEX. Yeah, well, you look the same. No Afro, but you look the same. Chuck, this is my wife, Freida.

CHUCK. David had Bathsheba and Alex has Freida. Beauty abounds.

ALEX. Hey, hey, watch it. No Bow-Wow stuff with the wives, that's the rule.

FREIDA. Thank you, Chuck. I like this Bow-Wow stuff already. Flatter me anytime. I don't hear it nearly enough.

CHUCK. That true, Alex?

ALEX. Believe me, I tell her how beautiful she is every day. That's my job, to keep her in a state of flattery.

FREIDA. Because he still believes it's going to get him everything.

CHUCK. Seems like it's got him something. Congratulations.

ALEX & FREIDA. Thank you.

ALEX. What have you been doing with yourself, man?

CHUCK. How much time do we have?

ALEX. What's it been—ten, twelve years?

CHUCK. That long? Well, you know I married Liz. Three girls: Maria twelve, Joy ten and Ebony seven.

ALEX. You know I never met your girls.

CHUCK. Yeah, I know.

DIANE. I wanted everybody to bring they kids, but Kirk figured since Sal and Bev—

ALEX. Yeah.

CHUCK. They're with Liz now anyway.

ALEX. Got kicked out of the ministry, Chuck? Come on, man.

CHUCK. Long, long involved story—

DIANE. Hmm.

CHUCK. Wasn't my fault.

DIANE. Hmm.

ALEX. So where's Liz?

CHUCK. I know you heard, she left me after all the controversy.

DIANE. Hmm.

CHUCK. OK, Dee. So I hear you guys are quite the academic couple.

FREIDA. Oh yeah, Mr. and Mrs. Tenure.

CHUCK. Wow, congratulations. I'll be up for mine some day.

ALEX. Man, let me tell you, Chuck, it ain't all it's cracked up to be, at least not where I'm at. Hey, maybe we should trade places.

CHUCK. No, I kind of like Howard University.

ALEX. What's not to like? Down in old Swanee—

CHUCK. Old Swanee?

FREIDA. That what he calls University of Georgia.

ALEX. I swear to you, man, the faculty and administration just turned in their white sheets and ropes for caps and gowns and computers.

CHUCK. Can't be that bad?

ALEX. I'm applying to Howard, my brother.

FREIDA. Wow, you guys act as if you haven't missed a beat.

CHUCK. It may not seem like it but I do keep up, Dee. Lester sends a postcard to my father's house every now and then, and when I go to New York, I always run into Luther.

ALEX. What's Luther doing?

DIANE. Nappy-head Luther ain't going nowhere but to the corner to drink some wine.

CHUCK. I tried to talk to him but he won't listen to me. And he doesn't even speak to Lester.

ALEX. But I bet you he talks about Lester on the corner with his drinking buddies, drinking that Wild Irish Rose. "That's right, Lester McMichael is too my brother." I can hear him now.

CHUCK. Luther is proud of Lester, but he won't let Lester give him anything. He says, "I don't take his advice so why should I take his money. I'm a man!" Then he adds other expletives which I choose not to repeat, takes a drink and goes about his business.

(KIRK enters dressed in a tank top and army fatigues.)

KIRK. Hey, Alex, you know this turkey lives right in D.C. and never calls anybody.

CHUCK. OK, I admit, my fault.

KIRK. You got that right. Gimme some money. *(He laughs.)* Chuck-onse! Alex-onse! *(KIRK hugs CHUCK, then ALEX. He kisses ALEX on the neck and cheek.)*

ALEX. Come on, Kirk! Damn. He still doing that?

(CHUCK laughs.)

KIRK. Well forgive me for living. I'm just glad to see ya, Bloop Blubber Bear!

ALEX. Freida, it's time to go home.

CHUCK. Not anymore, huh, Alex.

FREIDA. What did he call you?

ALEX. See, that's exactly why I didn't want to come here. Freida, you don't want to hear about that.

KIRK. You want to tell her about Bloop Blubber Bear, Chuck?

CHUCK. I don't think Alex wants to talk about that, Kirk.

KIRK. That's all right. If Lester was here he would help me tell the story of "some of us got it some of us don't." Wait a minute.

ALEX. Ah, come on, man.

KIRK. Sal! Hey, Sal! Hey, Sal! Get your behind up! Sal, come in here for a minute.

DIANE. They sleeping, Kirk.

KIRK. I don't care if they sleeping. They kept everybody else up last night. Hey, Sal!

ALEX. Freida. We going home.

CHUCK. Forget about it, Kirk.

KIRK. OK, OK, I won't say nothing.

FREIDA. I want to hear this.

ALEX. Freida, I'll tell you about it another time.

KIRK. Naw. Naw. See, you'll tell her your version and your version won't be the true version. Freida, I guarantee you our version is much better. It's like the difference between black and white, and Turnervision. Don't nobody want to see that colorized crap when you talking about the classics, and this is a classic. I like my Humphrey Bogart in black and white. Give me some money. *(He and FREIDA slap five.)*

DIANE. Kirk, you need to leave Alex alone.

ALEX. We are not talking about Humphrey Bogart. We are talking about me.

FREIDA. I want to hear the story.

(SAL enters. He is sleepy and hung-over.)

SAL. Yeah. What's up, Kirk? Oh shit—Chuck! *(The two men hug.)* I ain't seen this nigger in what, five years.

CHUCK. Six, right after my divorce.

SAL. You might be hearing about mine next. Kirk, you having army flashbacks, what's with all the rebely, man? Damn my head hurts.

KIRK. Freida wants to hear the story of Bloop Blubber Bear.

SAL. "Some of us got it some of us don't."

(ALEX gets up to leave, KIRK grabs him and sits him down. SAL grabs a beer from the fridge.)

KIRK. I wish Lester was here.

ALEX. Good idea. Why don't you wait until Lester gets here.

SAL. No, Alex. Hangover and all, I got this from the beginning.

KIRK. I love this. *(He laughs.)*

SAL. See, Rita—

FREIDA. Freida.

SAL. Yeah well anyway, all of us used to live in the same building. He tell you that?

FREIDA. No.

SAL. Me and Alex became friends first. Ninth grade.

CHUCK. Ninth grade. Wow.

SAL. So Lester and Chuck was best friends, right? Every morning we would run into Chuck and Lester on the elevator. Lester and Chuck used to tease me and Alex be-

cause, to be honest with you, at that time, me and Alex
was two of the nerdiest nerds you ever wanted to meet.
Both of us used to wear thick glasses, and Alex weighed
about three hundred pounds.

ALEX. Two hundred and thirty-eight, thank you.

SAL. Anyway, they called me Hawk Man because I used
to have a hook nose.

KIRK. Yep, remember that, Chuck?

CHUCK. Oh yeah.

SAL. Got my nose broke playing football when I was ten.

KIRK. He got it fixed though. Never will forget that time
we came to see you in the hospital. Yep.

SAL. Chuck started it. He started calling Alex Bloop Blubber Bear, after the cartoon character.

FREIDA (*holds back laughter*). Yes.

ALEX. OK, y'all having fun yet?

KIRK. See it's not how he got the name but how he got rid
of it.

ALEX. Shit.

SAL. I don't remember exactly how it happened but our
little group became known for having a lot of girlfriends.

KIRK. I know how it happened. We was some lovers,
that's how it happened. You better believe that. Gimme
some money.

DIANE. Humph.

FREIDA. Really?

DIANE. They was a mess. Stuck-up and conceited is what
they were. You couldn't tell them nothing.

KIRK. Shoot, that's 'cause we had it like that.

CHUCK. No. Everybody thought we were stuck-up and
conceited because we lived in Esplanade Gardens. You
have to picture beautiful, twenty-seven story Esplanade

Gardens, at the end of Lenox Avenue, surrounded by rundown tenements. Our families represented the black middle class. The other kids thought our families had money.

KIRK. They used to call us the rich kids.

CHUCK. Tell my mother and father that. My mother used to clean out offices at night just to make ends meet.

KIRK. They all stayed together though. All of 'em. The only thing separated any of our parents was death, bless they souls.

CHUCK. To get away from the neighborhood we would get on the subway—

KIRK. The iron horse was our Rolls Royce.

CHUCK. —and travel to Bedford, Stuyvesant or Brownsville Brooklyn, Staten Island, Hollis and Jamaica Queens, the South Bronx, searching for girls to meet. Praise God.

DIANE. On the prowl is what they was.

KIRK. Shoot, outside of sports that was our recreation. Kept us out of trouble, I'll tell you that.

ALEX. Got us in trouble too.

CHUCK. Freida, I don't know if Alex told you, but in our neighborhood we learned early that there were four ways you got respect. You could be good in sports, that was Sal and Kirk, you could fight, that was Sal.

KIRK. And you too, don't be modest, shoot, all of us could kick some bootie.

CHUCK. And you could have style, that was Lester, and I'll admit myself, you could hustle, that was Alex and Lester, or you could be a Casanova—Don Juan, and all of us thought we were that.

KIRK. Thought. Shoot, we was. Naturally, all the girls around the way usta get jealous.

FREIDA. Naturally.

SAL. Who was it that started calling us dogs?

CHUCK. Linda Hines.

KIRK. Oh yeah. I wonder whatever happened to her?

DIANE. Why?

KIRK. Aw, snookum-ookum, I was just wondering.

DIANE. Well don't be wondering. Next thing you know you be wanting, and I'm gonna tell you now you ain't having.

KIRK. Aw, snookum-ookum still loves me to death.

DIANE. Get away from me.

SAL. Girls would come to visit us from Brooklyn, Queens, the Bronx, and Manhattan.

KIRK. Lower east side. West side.

SAL. So naturally by the time we was sixteen all of us had lost our virginity.

KIRK. Shoot, more than twice.

SAL & KIRK. Except Alex.

ALEX. That's it. I'm outta here!

CHUCK. It's nothing to be proud of, Freida. But that's how we got the name the Bow-Wow Club.

KIRK. You got that right. Gimme some money.

SAL. But good old Alex couldn't be an official member of the Bow-Wow Club until he got laid.

DIANE. Alex, you can go in the living room if you don't want to listen to this mess, because I know I don't want to listen to it. I'll join you.

KIRK. Oh no. Y'all got to stay for the punch line. (He laughs.)

SAL. We knew this older woman, right, who was a nympho. She used to give everybody some.

DIANE. Old nasty thing.

KIRK. Karen French, that was her name.

ALEX. AWWWW!

SAL. One day I went over to her house, and asked her to do us a little favor. We went and got Alex, but nobody told him where we was going.

KIRK. What did you think that day, Alex?

ALEX. Frankly, Kirk, I don't remember.

SAL. Or do you choose to forget? We got to the house and she opens the door. Now you had to see this. She was wearing this see-through nightgown.

DIANE. Probably was all funky.

KIRK. Shoot, Karen was kinda fine!

DIANE. I knew her too. She was hardly fine—

CHUCK. She had some big, well you know, things, I remember that.

SAL. Shit, them "things" hit her knees when she didn't have her bra on. You remember that, Alex?

ALEX. Yes I do, thank you.

SAL. Anyway, we all go sit in the living room. She brings out some M.D. twenty/twenty and some reefer.

CHUCK. Wait a minute, Alex and I never touched any of that stuff. You guys were the lushes and the druggies.

SAL. You didn't need anything. Because everybody always thought you was on something.

CHUCK. It's called a natural high.

SAL. It's called silly.

CHUCK. You call it silly?

KIRK. You was, man. You used to laugh at everybody on the street who looked weird. If a retarded person walked down the street you used to imitate them and laugh. That's why it was a shock to everybody when you got religion.

CHUCK. God does have a sense of humor, doesn't he.

SAL. Anyway, she went into the bedroom, right. We told Alex to go into the bedroom.

ALEX. AW, MAN!

(FREIDA laughs.)

SAL. She closes the door, but we propped the door open just enough so we could see.

FREIDA *(laughing)*. That's horrible. Poor baby.

SAL *(demonstrating)*. Alex's big behind was going up and down.

CHUCK. While she was smoking a cigarette and chewing gum. Sorry, Alex, but it was a sight to behold.

SAL. When he was finished—

KIRK. In two minutes—

SAL. We all ran back into the living room and played like we didn't see nothing. Then Alex comes out of the room zipping up his pants and holding back this stupid smile. He rubs his chest and said:

SAL, CHUCK & KIRK. Some of us got it. Some of us don't! *(They all laugh hysterically.)*

ALEX. That's it, Freida, let's go home.

CHUCK. Then he rubbed his chest and said, y'all can't call me bloop blubber bear anymore, it's fate, call me:

SAL, CHUCK & KIRK. ALEXANDER THE GREAT!

(ALEX gets up to leave. Everyone in the room is laughing hard, even DIANE. FREIDA holds him.)

FREIDA. I knew there was something fishy about it every time you said, baby, I'm Alexander the Great. I kept saying to myself, I know he's not comparing himself to the Greek Alexander.

ALEX. Well, now you know. And it made sense to me. That's what she said, I was great, so I kept it.

(More laughter.)

FREIDA. Alex, you are great. You are. *(She kisses ALEX long and passionately.)*

ALEX. See, some of us got it, some of us don't.

(The sound of a beautiful baritone is heard singing "Summertime Baby." BEV enters followed by LESTER and LOITA. BEV is in a house gown. LESTER is dressed impeccably. LOITA wears a sexy, revealing outfit. As LESTER sings and dances, LOITA does an MTV groove dance.)

LESTER.

Well, it's the summertime baby,
you're on my case again.
It's the summertime baby,
you're on my case again.
Marrying and one woman just ain't my bag.
Please let me go, baby, I don't want to make you
**   feel sad.**
I told you last summer it was a one-summer thing
I'm looking this summer for a one-summer fling.
One-summer fling. one-summer fling. one-summer
**   fling.**

(KIRK leaps up and jumps into LESTER's arms.)

KIRK. Lester-onse!

LESTER. Kirk-onse, Sal-onse, Chuck-onse, Alex-onse, Dee-ette-onse! Bev-ette-onse!

FREIDA. Freida.

LESTER & KIRK. Freida-ette-onse!

(They all hug then LESTER breaks into a step which they all know and follow.)

THE MEN.
> **Ruff! Ruff!**
> **The Bow-Wow Club—ruff, ruff**
> **The Bow-Wow club—ruff, ruff**
> **The Bow-Wow club—ruff, ruff.**

(They stop and hug again, howling and acting like canines. The doorbell rings. BEV goes to the door.)

LESTER. The Bow-Wow Club. I told Snoop Doggy Dog, at the *Soul Train* awards, that he might not know it, but they are not the original dog pound. And if they wanted to learn something he should talk to some old-timers like us. Talking about a dog pound!

KIRK. And you know what? I said the same thing to them damn Q-shi-phi's, at Morgan State. Because we are the original, ruff-ruff—

LESTER *(breaks out into a rap).*
> **Once upon the time as the story is told**
> **There lived five guys that were**
> **Pretty black and bold**
> **They came from the ghetto**

That's nothing strange.
They earned prestige just the same,
They were,
The Bow-Wow Club.
Ruff, ruff
The Bow-Wow Club

THE MEN.
The Bow-Wow Club, ruff, ruff.

LESTER.
First there was Chuck who was heavy
and deep, had all the girls saying
"Oh he's so sweet."

(They all hug, again. Everyone is exuberant, They high-five, low-five, laugh, etc. BEV enters with PERRY.)

CHUCK. Hey, Perry. Everybody, this is Perry. Perry, this is everybody. Perry is, well, Perry is my, *my* significant other, my lover.

(They all look at one another in amazement, as fire-crackers go off. The light fades.)

SCENE THREE

(It is a half-hour later. The group, with the exception of CHUCK, PERRY and SAL, are in the living room. Lights up in the guest room. PERRY unpacks some clothes as CHUCK changes. Laughter comes from the living room.)

KIRK (*from the living room*). Hey, Chuck, come in here
    for a minute!

CHUCK. Be right there.

PERRY. I don't believe you didn't tell them. How could
    you do that to me?

CHUCK. I tried, Perry, I—

PERRY. Tried, what is there to try, Chuck, you just pick
    up the phone and say, I know I haven't seen any of you
    in a long time, there have been some changes in my
    life—

CHUCK. It's just not that easy

PERRY. Oh, but it's easy for you to have me come all the
    way out here to be fed to the lions.

CHUCK. No, Perry. When I talked to Dee, I got all choked
    up, I started sweating, you don't understand, this is not
    like telling your mother or your father.

PERRY. How would you know, you haven't even told them.

CHUCK. I know.

PERRY. Maybe they should have been first.

CHUCK. I haven't seen them in a long time, but they are
    more like my family than my family. If they accept this,
    then my biological family will accept it. The first thing
    my father would say is "How Lester and Sal feel about
    it?"

PERRY. We have been through this, Chuck. What if Lester
    and Sal think it's disgusting, foul, dirty, and that you are
    a degenerate, does that mean your father won't accept
    you? Oh God, what's with this acceptance stuff anyway.
    It's overrated. Who needs it? Maybe I'm being a little
    selfish here. Everybody knew I was gay before I hit pu-
    berty.

CHUCK. Well obviously it was a lot different for me.

PERRY. Obviously. When you asked me to come with you, I thought, Oh, God, does he know what he's getting into? I've been through these before and it's never easy, Chuck, but now you decided to surprise everybody, including me. I'm telling you I have a bad feeling about this one.

CHUCK. You get bad feelings about not getting a hard-on in the morning.

PERRY. That's not funny. This park we are going to? Are they going to carry rifles and go hunting? If they are I'm going home. I don't want to turn out like Burt Reynolds in *Deliverance*.

CHUCK. Don't be ridiculous! They are my friends, they are not murderers.

PERRY. If looks could kill they would be.

CHUCK. All I need is your support at my little coming-out party.

PERRY. If you wanted a coming-out party you should have told me and I would have arranged to have the party at my house. At least we could have invited some of our friends. Then we would have had home-court advantage.

CHUCK. Maybe you're right. But I figured since everybody is going to be here, it would be easier.

PERRY. So what are we going to do?

CHUCK. We are going to go downstairs and have a good time. They're really not that bad, you know.

PERRY. Coming-out parties are always the same. Shocking! It's better than going to a B horror movie. Shock, doom, denial.

CHUCK. Did you see Kirk and Alex? Talk about denial.

PERRY. Please don't leave the women out. I can tell Dee is a sweetheart, but the poor woman couldn't speak in a complete sentence: "Chuck, oh I'm sorry, I'm your, name is, I'm Kirk, I mean Dee, Chuck!

CHUCK *(laughs)*. I love them so much but those were some shocked and funny faces, weren't they?

PERRY. Try the Rocky Horror Picture Show. But that Lester is gorgeous. There is something about his aura that's— *(Sighs.)* You know I have all of his albums.

CHUCK. Of course I know. I brought them.

PERRY. I brought the "Funky Melody" C.D.

CHUCK. Wow, that one. When Lester sings, it's like he's singing to you, and you alone. He's one of the few people I know who truly loves people.

PERRY. That's cute. I never met a real star before. But that macho dick, aggh. Did you see the look he gave me?

CHUCK. That's Sal. He was always the hothead, always! One time, we were at a party in the Eden Wall projects in the Bronx. Black Spade territory.

KIRK *(from living room)*. Hey, Chuck!

PERRY. Black Spade territory?

CHUCK. Be right there! They were the baddest street gang in New York City.

PERRY. The only black spades I recall were in a deck of cards, and those hunks that hung out on the pier in black leather jackets—they were kind of scary but that's what made it exciting.

CHUCK. Those days are over, I hope.

PERRY. They are. Have to be careful these days, and besides I have you now.

(CHUCK attempts to kiss PERRY. PERRY moves away.)

PERRY. I'm still angry about this little situation, you know.

CHUCK. Perry, please—

PERRY. Tell me about the Black Spades. Really give me a reason to be afraid. Very, very afraid.

CHUCK. Some girl we met invited us to the party. I'll never forget, "Betcha By Golly Wow," by Stylistics was playing. The red lights were on, and I was grindin' this girl down to the floor. One of those deep, slow knee grinds.

PERRY. I wish I could have seen that. On second thought—

CHUCK. All of a sudden the party was crashed by a group of Black Spades. Apparently I was dancing with one of their girlfriends.

PERRY. What happened?

CHUCK. They just told us to get out, but Sal says f-y'all, and the next thing you know, people are being hit with chains, baseball bats, bullets started flying. I think Alex and Lester still have scars to show for that one. But somehow the Lord allowed us to get out of there. We got split up but we all got home. The funny part about the whole thing was, it was four in the morning. We all had twelve o'clock curfews and our parents were up waiting for us to get home. Lester's parents called the police. Sal's father was up reading the Bible. Alex's father locked him out so his mother left a cheese sandwich on the staircase. They kept that up for a week. Poor Kirk might have been better off facing the Black Spades than getting the beating he took from his father. Mr. Bright's fifteen minutes of fame came from being knocked out by Sonny Liston. God rest his soul. "Spare the rod, spoil the child." And my mother wasn't much better. I tried to sneak into the apartment, and she was standing behind the door with her high-heel shoe. Put holes and knots all over my head. Here we were claiming our manhood while our parents are up waiting for us to come home.

PERRY. My mother still waits for me to come home, you know that. They sound a bit scary, and a bit phobic—

CHUCK. Do they sound a bit black?

PERRY. Chuck, you know me better than that.

CHUCK. I'm just nervous, that's all. Perry, I promise it will be fine. If not, we will leave—

KIRK (*from the living room*). HEY, CHUCK!

PERRY. Be right there! We better go before they think we're doing something funny.

CHUCK. Perry, I need this. Remember when I thought I was sick?

PERRY. Why do you want to bring that up?

CHUCK. All I could think about was the Bow-Wow Club. I'd just remember us walking down Seventh Avenue. Seventeen years old. Wild and crazy, flop hats, and tip-it hats, marshmallow shoes, pressed Lee jeans, blyes, alpacas. We thought we were immortal. I'll never forget that line from Cooley High, when that teacher, played by Garret Morris, asked Preach, the Glynn Thurman character, what he wanted in life, and Preach looked at him a long time, and said, "I want to live forever." That was us. Nobody ever said it, but at that time we knew we'd live forever. And that was my first contact with the God. How else can anybody live forever. I prayed for all of us to live forever. Perry, I'm scared. That's why I'm glad you are here. Now let me worry about them. And you just look out for me. OK?

PERRY. I am still mad at you, you know. *(PERRY kisses CHUCK as lights fade.)*

(Laughter comes from the living room as lights fade in the bedroom. Lights come up. LESTER has given BEV a designer valise. There are packages on the sofa and the floor. ALEX holds an African mask trimmed in ivory. KIRK has a 14-karat gold football. DIANE has a 14-karat gold chain.)

BEV. Shoot, they gonna have to give me my own T.V. series now. Forget *Law and Order*, try *Beverly D.A.*, she always gets her man. Get it? Man? Always. I could put a whole lot of briefs in here. Got it? Briefs? Motions and lotions. *(She walks with her valise like a sexy model. She turns and gives that television look. Everybody laughs.)*

LOITA. Bat your eyes, throw your hair back, position your lips like this. *(LOITA gives a sexy movement with her lips.)*

BEV. Baby, I can bat my eyes and throw my hair, but I'm not doing my lips like that. I am not trying to be Farrah Fawcett or somebody, just Beverly D.A. Thank you, Lester. This is so sweet. Now I have to pass the bar, or I am going have to give this back.

DIANE. You know you gonna pass that bar, girl.

(They high-five each other.)

KIRK. Getting loose, ain't you, Dee!

DIANE. Shoot, I'm having fun.

(They all laugh.)

LESTER. Where is that Sal?

BEV. Why you want to go and spoil everything, Lester?

KIRK. Said he was going back to sleep.

ALEX. I thought I saw him walk out of the door.

BEV. Wherever he is, let him stay there.

KIRK. Hey, Chuck! Chuck! Come in here and get your gift, man.

(LOITA gives FREIDA a gift.)

FREIDA. Oh no. No, I can't.

ALEX. Open the gift, Freida. I want to see what it is.

(She opens the gift. It is a kinte cloth gown.)

EVERYBODY. WOW!

LOITA. I picked it out?

DIANE *(holding a string of pearls)*. You didn't have to do this, Lester.

(FREIDA kisses LESTER and LOITA on the cheek.)

KIRK. That's right, Lester, you didn't have to do this, but on second thought, since he got it like that, shoot, gimme some money.

DIANE. Kirk—

KIRK. You know what I mean, but on third thought, I did put a whole lot of money into the house and—

DIANE. Kirk—

KIRK. Justice and Bobby almost ready to go to college.

LESTER, ALEX, BEV & DIANE. College!

KIRK. I'm only joking around, Lester.

LESTER. College? Good Lord, does that make me feel old—

BEV. That's because we are old.

KIRK. Y'all may be old, but I ain't old—

BEV. I know I better hurry up and pass this bar. I can't imagine being in school the same time as Justice—

(They all laugh as PERRY and CHUCK enter.)

CHUCK. I didn't know we were exchanging gifts.

LESTER. Just a little something to show how much I miss you guys. Here.

LOITA *(gives CHUCK a small box)*. You should have seen Lester. When we were in Paree, he was like a child picking out the gifts. We had to wait to come to New York to get this one for Chucky.

(She looks at LESTER and winks. CHUCK opens the box It is a Timex.)

CHUCK. Oh, no.

LESTER. Huh?

KIRK. What is it?

CHUCK. A Timex. The exact same Timex.

ALEX & KIRK. Let me see it.

(CHUCK hands the Timex to KIRK who examines it.)

KIRK. Hello!

BEV. Let me see it too!

ALEX. Now this brings back memories I can talk about.

PERRY. I feel a story coming.

FREIDA. Funny, I get that same feeling.

CHUCK. Thanks, man.

LESTER. I wish Sal would come on.

BEV. Please don't, cutie pie. Look at Lester. He still cute, isn't he, Dee?

DIANE. Wouldn't know it by those C.D. covers. With all that makeup. They can't make you look like yourself?

LESTER. Well—

DIANE. 'Cause you sure look better than that, what that's one?

BEV. The "Funky Melody" C.D.

LESTER. Oh, that one. I didn't even recognize myself. I was—where was I? Oh, Germany, and I'm walking by this shop, and I see the hugest picture of this black face, nothing but teeth, though. I said to myself, Who is that? And somebody came up to me asking for my autograph.

BEV. You look a lot better than your pictures. I want you to know that.

DIANE. Yep. Somebody would have thought you was trying to hide something under all that makeup.

LOITA. Lester always looks very fine.

KIRK. All right. All right. That's enough. Shoot. I'm not cute.

(No one responds.)

CHUCK. Where is Sal?

KIRK. I'm not cute?

ALEX. I don't think he took your news too well, Chuck.

PERRY. The proverbial understatement.

(FREIDA hits PERRY playfully.)

ALEX. I'm not cute?

CHUCK. I figured Sal would have a hard time with it.

KIRK. I'm not cute?

LESTER, DIANE, BEV & ALEX. Yes, Kirk, you are cute!

KIRK. All right then. Gimme some money. *(He slaps five with the closest person.)*

CHUCK *(changing focus)*. Lester, the big star.

LESTER. This weekend, I am just one of the fellows of the original Bow-Wow Club. Man, you don't know. I get so tired of it all, y'all. The traveling, the airplanes, the crowds, the phony people, the racism.

KIRK. But you got to admit, it's better than the alternative.

LESTER. What's the alternative?

KIRK. That you never made it.

LESTER. Sometimes I wonder, man.

KIRK. See, it's easy to think that way now, but, man, if you was out here struggling like us, you would be dreaming of doing exactly what you doing now. You are living your dream, man. Not many people get a chance to do that. They say people don't know what they have until they lose it, don't let that happen to you. Easier coming down than it is going up.

LESTER. Don't get me wrong, I'm not trying to lose anything. In fact, I have to work even harder to stay where I am. I work hard just like anybody else in this room.

KIRK. But you love what you do. You got talent. You think I loved being in the army? Kiss my bootie. It was all right at first, but they stopped seeing me when I proved I could move up the ladder like anybody else, and when they stopped seeing me, I stopped seeing the point of being in the army. So my question to you is, do you still love it?

LESTER. Geraldo Rivera over here. Yeah, I still love it, I guess. Dee, you been letting him watch too many talk shows in his retirement.

ALEX. Kirk always talked that talk. How do you think he got into the Bow-Wow Club? Sure wasn't because he was cute.

KIRK. I beg to differ.

CHUCK. I remember Kirk used to get a woman in a corner at a party and trap her there.

ALEX. Wouldn't let her go for the whole night, breaking her down.

LESTER. Be up in the woman's face like this. *(Demonstrates.)*

KIRK. You got that right. But you better believe I always came away with at least two or three phone numbers too. Shoot, sometimes I got more than that.

DIANE *(elbows KIRK)*. All right, you getting carried away.

PERRY. I'm curious. Could we hear the watch story?

LOITA. I know the watch story.

DIANE & BEV. I bet you do.

BEV *(to DIANE, then to LOITA)*. And a few other stories too. Baby, how long have you and Lester been together?

LESTER. What is it now?

LOITA. Ahh, six months.

BEV. You go booy!

DIANE & BEV. That's a long time for you, isn't it, Lester?

KIRK. Diane! I call her Diane when she leaves her home training out in the yard. *(Laughs.)*

DIANE. All right, you can go right out in the yard with my home training.

LOITA. Six months is very long for me too. I never went out with anyone for more than, let's say two months.

BEV. Well excuse me.

LESTER. Loita may be the one, fellas. *(He and LOITA kiss long and passionately.)*

BEV. Getting a little hot in here.

KIRK. Lester-onse!

ALEX. That's nice.

DIANE. HUMPH!

LESTER *(finally breaking the embrace)*. Yeah, Loita knows all about us. I bet she could tell the watch story. You want to try?

LOITA. The watch story.

PERRY. Drum roll, please. *(PERRY drums his fingers on the table. They all look at him as if he is crazy.)*

LESTER. The watch story as told by Loita. *(He gives a drum roll.)*

LOITA. OK, let me see, once upon a time there was a boy.

BEV. Oh, Lord.

KIRK. A very strange and enchanted boy.

CHUCK. Kirk, she's telling my story.

PERRY. He's right, strange and enchanted, boy. I like that.

LOITA. His name was Chuck, and he had a best friend. His name was Lester.

KIRK. It was the best of times, it was the worst of times.

ALEX & DIANE. Kirk!

LOITA. It was Chuck's fifteenth birthday?

CHUCK. Fifteenth.

LOITA. So his father brought a birthday gift, a watch.

LESTER. A gold-plated Timex watch.

KIRK. Can't leave that part out. Mercy!

LOITA. A gold-plated Timex watch. The two boys went on a shopping spree to celebrate Chuck's birthday with—

LESTER. Forty-two dollars and fifty cents.

KIRK. Neighborhood Youth Corp Jobs, love those democrats!

BEV. Long time since then, huh, Lester?

KIRK. You got that right, gimme some money.

LOITA. The store, the name, I am not so good here—

LESTER. Help her out, Chuck!

CHUCK (*enjoying the story*). E.J. Korvette's

EVERYBODY. E.J. Korvette's!!

LOITA. E.J. Kor— Korvette, department store.

DIANE. On 34th Street and Broadway.

BEV. That's where y'all brought those ugly-looking print shirts. Remember those, Dee?

DIANE. Do I.

ALEX. Korvette's. Shoulda been shopping uptown at A.J. Lester's, keep the money in the community.

LESTER. Look who's talking. Your favorite store back then was Alexander's. What was your excuse?

KIRK, CHUCK & LESTER. "Man I got stock in that store, that's why it's got my name."

ALEX. I can't be held responsible for that.

LESTER. Oh. And we can? Check him out.

DIANE. Y'all know all those stores went under. Alexander's and Korvette's. But you can get some of the same stuff on the Home Shopping Network. (*Pause.*)

ALEX. I'm just showing y'all how indoctrinated and brainwashed we were, and still are.

LOITA. May I finish the story, please?

ALEX. Excuse me, Loita. I just get a little hyped up about all this. (*Short pause.*)

LOITA. So, Chucky and Lester leave the Korvette's, with shopping bags in hand, and standing in front the E.J. Korvette are two girls, who were a vision to their eyes!

LESTER. That's right, Regina and Chuck's future wife, Liz.

LOITA. So the two boys go to the two girls in the Bow-Wow style.

(Imitating how LESTER would have said it. LESTER says this along with her.)

LOITA & LESTER. "Excuse me, sweetheart, but you look like you need a bodyguard, as beautiful as you are. You are like a—

LOITA. —walking treasure chest with gold, diamonds, rubies, and pearls.

LESTER. You are like gold wrapped in chocolate, and I know your thighs must be sweet honey because my sweet tooth is aching and my body is shaking just because your essence is invading my presence—

CHUCK, LOITA & LESTER. —with sweetness and greediness, with a need to have you in my arms.

LESTER. Just call me Black Les, the pirate. I'll be your insurance against all who—

CHUCK & LESTER —want to pillage your beauty. I'll take care of your every need—mentally, emotionally and physically.

LESTER, KIRK & CHUCK. I'll be like Mutual of Harlem, and you can be my Blue Cross Blue Shield—that way both of our backs are covered." *(The group laughs hard.)*

FREIDA. Girls fell for that?

LESTER & KIRK. The sweet nothings worked every time!
(They slap five.)

ALEX. You woulda fell for it too—

FREIDA. Alex Earle, if you would have come to me with a line like that, we would not be sitting here right now, because I wouldn't have given you the time of day. I promise you that.

ALEX. We were teenagers, Freida.

FREIDA. Then too.

LESTER & KIRK. Yeah, right!

CHUCK. Girls fell for it, Freida.

FREIDA. I am dying to hear what your line was, Chuck.

PERRY. So am I?

KIRK. I used Kahlil Gibran, myself. Give me some money.

(He turns to the nearest person, which is PERRY, and slaps five. PERRY doesn't know the slap. KIRK gets on his knees and recites a few lines of Kahlil Gibran to DI-ANE.)

"How often have you sailed in my dreams. And now you come in my awakening, which is my deeper dream. Ready I am to go and my sails full set awaits the wind." And—um—um—oh yeah, "And then I shall come to you, a boundless drop to a boundless ocean."

DIANE. Shut up, Kirk!

KIRK. You married me, didn't you?

CHUCK, LESTER, BEV & ALEX. Oops!

DIANE. I ain't thinking about y'all.

LOITA. Lester said Chuck and Sal didn't have to have lines because they had the huge Afro's.

FREIDA. Yes, and—

LOITA. You will have to explain that one.

LESTER. Chuck and Sal had these huge Afro's, like the Jackson Five or Black Ivory, and if you had a big Afro, you didn't have to say anything but—

CHUCK. Hi, my name is Chuck, what's your name?

ALEX. Y'all see how deep that shit is?

LESTER. What now, Alex?

FREIDA. Alex.

ALEX. Even during the heart of the civil rights movement. Black is beautiful and all that, white consciousness still had us wrapped by the balls. They were still telling us who we were supposed to be attracted to.

BEV. Oh, no. You have got to explain this one.

ALEX. If you got black hair, kinky kinks. You ain't gonna have a big Afro, blowing in the wind and shit. You don't see any Africans with big Afros blowing in the wind. But if your hair is mixed with that European stock or Latin stock or Asian stock, then your hair is going to be longer, it's going to have that bounce. I don't know how many times I got turned down back then because I didn't have so-called good hair, or a Jackson Five-size Afro. If straight hair is good, then what's kinky hair—no good. Fucked up in the head, man, figuratively and literally.

(SAL appears in the archway. He stands and listens. He has a drink in his hand.)

DIANE. Alex, I didn't care how big an Afro was, if you didn't look good, a Afro wasn't going to hide it.

KIRK. Take me, for instance.

LESTER, ALEX & CHUCK. Yeah?

KIRK. Nothing.

BEV. I do know what you are saying, Alex, but you are not giving us enough credit. Like Diane said, ugly is ugly. Dark-skinned or light-skinned. A 'fro never made a difference to me. I used to like Caesars, anyway. Lester, didn't you wear a Caesar back then?

CHUCK & KIRK. Yeah, but Lester could sing.

CHUCK. All Lester had to do was doo-whoop-do-whoop.

KIRK. And panties was dropping.

CHUCK. I didn't say that.

ALEX. Missing the point. Black people are still messed up in the head, Bev. If you wore a Caesar you got more attention if it had waves in it. What do you need for waves? So-called good hair. In my African-American studies class down at Morehouse, all my black students watch videos. Who's presented as beautiful, the light-skinned women. "I want me a light-skinned woman. What's up light skin!" That self-hatred thing has been ingrained in us since they brought us over here on those boats.

FREIDA. Alex. Every day Alex comes home, he's got another horror story. We could be here all night listening to all the stories, right, Alex?

KIRK. Jeez, Alex, you gonna spoil all the fun this weekend, or what?

ALEX. That's why I don't like re-hashing the past, because I see how stupid I was. You might see it as fun but I see it from a different point of view.

LOITA. So!! They escort the girls home, however, Regina and Liz lived in za—

LESTER. —notorious St. Nicholas projects.

LOITA. I try to picture this place in my mind because Lester makes it sound so horrific.

KIRK. Horrific ain't the word. You walk into St. Nick you was taking your life in your hands even if you was minding your own business. Mike Lagrant and the Forty Thieves, would stab ya, shoot ya and carve their initials in you. Might burn you if they didn't like you.

LOITA. I believe the boys realized they were in for big trouble.

ALEX. Les and Chuck got off easy because y'all just got the clothes taken and shit slapped out of y'all.

KIRK. Right. But Chuck's face was the size of a grapefruit. And then— (KIRK laughs hard. He knows what's coming next.) Lester and Chuck go home, right.

CHUCK. Oh my God.

KIRK. When Mr. Hooter finds out, he told Chuck he had one of two choices.

LOITA. This is my favorite part. May I say the part?

PERRY. Is this true, Chuck?

KIRK. Every word of it, Percy!

LOITA (mimicking CHUCK's father). "Either you go back and get your watch, or you stay here and deal with me, and if you do that, it ain't gonna be a pretty sight."

KIRK. Oh, shoot, she sound just like Mr. Hooter.

LESTER. The week before, Mike Lagrant picked big Todd over his head and broke his back over a fire hydrant.

ALEX. Yeah, but remember when Mr. Hooter slapped that pimp named Sehan, from 43rd Street. I'd put my money on Mr. Hooter any day.

FREIDA. What a situation!

LESTER. A serious problem. We sat on that car in front of the building for hours. Chuck was thinking about running away from home. Then, Kirk, Sal and Alex showed up, and we sat there, and we sat there, until Sal says—

(SAL enters.)

SAL. Let's go get your fucking watch.

LESTER. Let's go get your fucking watch. *(He slaps five and hugs SAL.)*

LOITA. So the Bow-Wow Club!—

KIRK. —also known as the Lenox Avenue Five, and, the "Black Musketeers"—

LOITA. —go to the—

KIRK. Stroll to the St. Nick projects—

ALEX. Peeing in our pants. I'll never forget that. Lagrant was holding Liz by the arm like he had her on a leash. I'll be honest, I was scared that day.

BEV. And wasn't he wearing the watch?

CHUCK. Sure was.

LOITA. And that is when Chuck walks to this villain—

KIRK. Mike Lagrant—

LOITA. —and said to him—

KIRK. I love this! Chuck says—

CHUCK. "My father told me to come back and get my watch."

(Everyone laughs.)

KIRK. But while Lagrant stood there laughing, Chuck punched him in the face. His nose split like a broken ketchup bottle.

FREIDA. Did you get your watch back?

LESTER. We got our asses kicked!

ALEX. We got the watch back. It was busted up but he got it back.

CHUCK. Yeah. Timex may take a licking, but they don't always keep ticking.

KIRK. But everybody knew us after that. We got major respect. Nobody walked into St. Nick projects and demanded nothing, not even the police.

LESTER. Especially because their father said so.

(They all clap.)

CHUCK. Thanks, man.

LESTER. And this is for you.

(LOITA reaches into a bag and retrieves another box. CHUCK opens it and pulls out a Rolex watch.)

CHUCK. What, are you kidding, I can't take this?

PERRY. Yes, you can.

KIRK. Slap me, and tell me you kissed me, let me see.

(They pass the watch around.)

LOITA. Lester? Sal?

SAL. You know stories about me too?

LESTER. Hey, we do more than sit around talking about the Bow-Wow Club.

SAL. I wouldn't know about that. I don't know what to believe anymore, because you think you know somebody, then all of a sudden you find out you don't know a goddamn thing.

BEV. Sal.

SAL. You know what I figured out. I figured out that y'all some fake-ass motherfuckers, that's what I figured out. Lester comes in here playing like he's Santa Claus. Everybody know you a star, man, you don't have to rub it in.

LESTER. Sal, you know me better than that.

SAL. I thought I did, but what the fuck do I really know. And my main man, Chuck—we usta go to karate class together. Played basketball and football together. We did everything together. That time out in Queens, queens— when that girl's father let us spend the night because he thought it was too late to take the train back to Harlem—we slept in the same bed together. You even braided my hair for me. What about that time David Young pulled his pants down, and showed us his dick. David had a dick, man, that he had to pick up off the ground. What was you really thinking about when you saw that, Chuck?

BEV. Sal!

KIRK. Yo, Sal!

CHUCK. I actually came here to warn you about that night in Queens, Sal. Something could have rubbed off on you, a delayed reaction. Be careful, your voice might get a little higher any minute now.

PERRY. Good for you, Chuck. Point.

SAL. Don't play with me, man!

PERRY. Oh boy.

KIRK. I'm just about to go get my pistol!

BEV. I'm about to go home.

SAL. You ain't going home. I'm going home.

BEV. Well if you going home I'm not going home, because the whole idea is to get away from you!

KIRK. Attention!

SAL. Ain't nobody here in the goddamn army! Damn! Chuck a faggot, got the nerve to walk in here with another faggot, and a white faggot.

PERRY. I knew I was a faggot, but I'm white! I'll remember next time I fill out a job application.

CHUCK. Nobody here is a faggot, Sal.

SAL. That's what you said you are. You said so, man, or whatever. I mean, if somebody woulda come to me and told me my main boy was a fag, I woulda kicked they ass defending you, but you said it yourself: "This is my significant other." In my book that makes you a fag. Maybe I oughta kick your ass.

ALEX. Wait a minute. Nobody is kicking nobody's ass, all right?

(LESTER, KIRK and ALEX stand ready to stop SAL.)

PERRY. I know sometimes people suffer from stunted growth, so he's got to be twelve, right?

SAL. Did you say something to me? Now I got to listen to this whiny sarcastic bastard.

ALEX & LESTER. Yo, Sal!

KIRK. Sal!

SAL. Say something, so I can knock the fay out of you.

(He makes a move toward PERRY. ALEX and KIRK stop him. SAL stumbles and falls.)

SAL *(on the floor)*. The Bow-Wow Club ain't shit!

BEV. Sal, you are drunk off your ass.

SAL *(trying to get up)*. You goddamn right I'm drunk, and I'll kick every motherfucker's ass in here. Y'all couldn't stop me when I was seventeen. What makes you think y'all can do it now!

KIRK. Sal, you have got to respect my wife, my house and my guest, man.

SAL. Oh, I'm not your guest too? Lester didn't disrespect me? Coming in here flirting with my wife. And you ain't keeping that book bag either. Showing off!

LESTER & BEV. What?

SAL. Fuck y'all. I'm going home. I don't want to be around a bunch of flakes. *(SAL walks. He is so drunk he stumbles.)*

ALEX. You are not driving anywhere. You need to sleep it off. That's what you need to do.

LESTER. Sal—

SAL *(on the floor)*. Invite me back when the faggot and the star ain't here.

PERRY. Do we have to take this?

KIRK. He's drunk, um—Percy. *(To SAL.)* I'm gonna help you to the bedroom. *(To everybody in the room.)* Let him sleep it off before we go to the lake.

SAL. I don't need no bedroom. Make sure you lock my door, godammit!

BEV. Chuck, I'm so sorry

(KIRK and SAL exit. BEV and DIANE follow them. After a moment:)

LESTER. Hey, y'all OK?

CHUCK. I didn't mean to come here and, man oh man—

LESTER. That's the liquor talking, you know he didn't mean it.

PERRY. Your family? Dysfunction runs amuck!

(Long pause. CHUCK paces. He is obviously upset.)

LESTER. Chuck, remember that time that barber put that relaxer in your hair?

CHUCK. Mr. Bob, yeah, I remember.

LOITA. Lester said you looked like Prince?

LESTER. Loita—

CHUCK. More like James Brown, before all my hair fell out.

LESTER. Remember that, Alex? I think about that sometimes before I go on the stage for some reason. It still makes me laugh. The look you had on your face that day, I'll never forget. I guess we can never take ourselves too seriously, huh. You are still Chuck to me, always will be. I love you, man.

(ALEX looks off in another direction.)

CHUCK. I love you too. Thanks, Lester.

LESTER. You're going to go in there and get ready to go to the lake, right?

CHUCK. I don't know. I don't know.

(PERRY storms out of the living room. CHUCK follows PERRY out.)

FREIDA. Poor guy.

ALEX. It's a hard thing to handle, him coming in here like that.

FREIDA. Alex, I thought you were going to leave this alone?

ALEX. I am.

LESTER. What are you saying, Alex?

ALEX. I wasn't going to say anything, but it becomes clearer to me every day.

FREIDA. Would you leave it alone then.

ALEX. They get us in all kinds of ways, Les. If it's not drugs, or alcohol, or prison, it's by something else. Chuck wasn't no homosexual.

LESTER. Who cares what he was. That is still Chuck in there. The same guy that used to call you Bloop Blubber Bear.

ALEX. Tell me about it. Think I liked that shit? Maybe I should call him Bloop Homo—Fomo!

FREIDA. Alex!

ALEX. See how he likes that.

FREIDA. Alex Earle! Lester, Alex is bringing his work into this wonderful reunion and I asked him not to do that. But sometimes he has a problem with what's appropriate and what's not.

LESTER. I see.

ALEX. I couldn't find a more appropriate situation then right now to support what I know is right. If you can't see that, then everybody in here is blind.

LESTER. Alex, that's the same guy that fought for you on the streets. Whose momma's pots you used to go into even when he couldn't. That's who that is. Who cares who he decides to be with? It isn't you.

ALEX. Lester, you've been in the music business too long. You accept too much. Just like you were saying, you don't like the business, but you are still in it. Why? Because you accept the bullshit so you can keep getting paid all that money.

LESTER. Alex, do you know what you are calling me?

ALEX. Yeah, you're a sellout! Look, I'm just saying, it's an attitude. And that attitude crosses over into every area of our lives, man. I can't just accept it. If you can, fine, but you have to realize that even in the music industry they come after us, and use us, and we don't even know it. All those songs we grew up with had nothing to do with teaching how to be real men. Every song, some dude is crying about some crazy chick that did him wrong: "Have You Seen Her?" "Ain't Too Proud to Beg," "It Takes a Fool," "Walk on By," "It Hurts So Bad." Come on, man, you ever listen to the words? Weak!

FREIDA. Alex, what am I going to do—that's enough!

LESTER. If you don't like my music, that's fine, man. Guess what? My last album sold over three million, so it doesn't really matter to me what you think. Am I supposed to give up my houses, my cars, my gold, diamonds and jewelry because you have a problem with the lyrics? Reality check, brother Alex, or are you so far gone into your Africanism that you can't see where the hell you are standing? And I don't need an answer to that. I'll tell you, you are standing in the new home of Kirk Bright, which happens to be in the home of the free, in the land of opportunity—

ALEX. They got you more brainwashed than I ever dreamed, man.

LESTER. Alex, I don't give a damn what you feel about me or my music, OK?

ALEX. Fine, brother.

LESTER. Now that we have established that, just for my knowledge, please make me understand what this problem is you have with Chuck.

ALEX. I can't just accept what he's doing with his life.

LESTER. His life!

ALEX. Man, do you know there were no faggots in Africa until them Europeans showed up.

FREIDA. Here we go.

LESTER. What?

ALEX. There is no history of homosexuality in Africa. Nobody knew about that shit until the Greeks. Believe me, Lester, I am an expert.

LESTER. It's really hard for me to sit here and listen to this. You really are stretching shit.

ALEX. Lester, it's a fact.

LESTER. You can't prove that! You sound like one of those white racists who claims that blacks are genetically inferior!

ALEX. Everybody with common sense knows that's not true because they can't prove it. What I'm saying can be proved.

LESTER. Oh jeez! I am not even going to ask how because it really doesn't make a difference. None of that has anything to do with Chuck and how you and Sal are treating him!

ALEX. Too far out in a star galaxy to understand—

LESTER. Freida, I know this is your husband, the two of you have a child coming into this world, I hope you don't allow him to raise that child with that attitude. Talking about attitude.

ALEX. What did you say?

LESTER. I'm apologizing for you, man.

ALEX. You don't need to apologize for me! This is my wife! You think she doesn't know me! Apologize for yourself! Look at you, walking in here all—never mind.

LESTER. All what?

ALEX. Nothing

LESTER. Alex, I thought I knew you—

ALEX. Walking in here all fucked up. You've been too busy being some white man's creation to know me.

FREIDA. Alex, if you don't stop, I am leaving! I'm serious, because I am feeling ill, right now. This is making me ill. I can't take anymore.

ALEX. I told you I didn't want to come here. Now you see why?

LESTER. Alex.

FREIDA. Go take a walk or something. We did not drive all the way from Atlanta, Georgia, for you to lecture everybody.

(ALEX exits through the front door.)

LESTER. Alex!

FREIDA. I have honestly never seen him this upset! Lester, I really apologize for him.

(LESTER exits.)

LOITA. Looks like you need a hug. You want a hug?

FREIDA. Yes, I do need a hug. *(They hug.)*

LOITA. Lester brought some firecrackers. He got them from Hong Kong. Don't ask me how he got them on the airplane. I don't know that one. You want to go outside and set some off?

FREIDA. I believe we have had enough fireworks for one day.

LOITA. Something about the firecrackers that makes me feel better. Something about blowing the things up. It's like power or something. That's why men get off on it so much, guns, the bombs, I like it, though. I like the feeling. The power.

FREIDA *(after a moment)*. Power. Loita, when I was a little girl I used to sneak out into the woods by my parents house and sit under this big oak tree and read books on Angela Davis, Assata Shakkur, Bella Abzug. Those women had no problem taking control of a situation, whether it was dazzling people with beauty and intelligence, knocking a man out or blowing things up. My parents thought I was crazy when I used to quote them at the supper table. I used to imagine myself going with them on the fight for humanity. It was like going on the quest for the Holy Grail or something. Peace and love on earth, man.

LOITA. I never heard of them.

FREIDA. No. Let me tell you all about these women. Firecrackers, huh?

LOITA. Lester's got ash cans, Roman rockets, cherry bombs, sizzlers, sparklers.

FREIDA. Yes, you know, Loita, I feel like blowing something or someone up right now.

LOITA. Bangers, the M-80s—

(As they exit, lights fade.)

END OF ACT ONE

ACT TWO

SCENE ONE

(Lights come up on DIANE, BEV, LESTER and ALEX at the campsite. They are eating hot dogs, hamburgers, steaks and ribs, fried chicken, along with other side dishes. Bottles of alcohol are on the table. There are two picnic tables and a tree. The background should give the indication of the woods. There should be a portable C.D. player, backgammon set, football, and cards. DIANE and BEV barbecue. Off in the distance we hear LOITA and FREIDA setting off firecrackers.)

LESTER. Whoa! This potato salad is slamming, Dee!

BEV. Sure is. I don't know why we had to come way out here to eat it though. Shoot, it's hot! And these mosquitoes won't leave me alone.

LESTER. That's because you got sweet blood. Mosquitoes like sugar.

BEV. You hear, Lester?

DIANE. He can't help hisself. He just a old dog.

LESTER. Ruff-ruff

DIANE & BEV. Down, boy. *(They laugh.)*

DIANE *(at the grill)*. I told Kirk I was going to end up barbecuing.

BEV. It's not his fault, Dee. Somebody had to wait for Sal to wake up and it wasn't going to be me, because one of us would end up dead.

LESTER. The Colonel better come and take some lessons because this fried chicken is kicking, too!

ALEX. Yeah. The fried chicken is good, huh?

BEV. Why do you want to know? You don't eat none. Hmmm, it's good.

LESTER. I like it out here: fresh air, good food, good friends, loved ones. You think Chuck decided not to come?

DIANE. He said he was coming.

BEV. Damn bugs. He had to follow Kirk's directions, who knows where they could be.

ALEX. I don't know how he could pull that on us.

LESTER. Look, we not gonna start this again.

ALEX. All right. Damn shame though.

LESTER. What?

ALEX. You know what?

LESTER. Alex, let me tell you something

ALEX. You can't tell me nothing.

DIANE. What is wrong with y'all!

BEV *(changing the subject)*. Too many bugs out here, y'all! I'm a Harlem girl. The only bugs I can tolerate is roaches. Anything else give me the heebiejeebies.

(An ash can goes off, scaring everyone.)

DIANE. I know it's the Fourth of July, but goodness gracious!

ALEX. Freida!

FREIDA *(offstage)*. We are OK, Alex. That was just an ash can!

BEV. Sound like an atomic bomb.

DIANE. And she got that baby too, Alex, I wouldn't let—

ALEX. Freida has got a mind of her own, Dee. She knows more about being pregnant than I do. *(A long silence as everyone looks at ALEX.)* I'm just saying she knows more—she knows more about her own body than I do.

BEV. We know exactly what you are saying, Alex—

LESTER. Man, when that baby starts crying at night it's not gonna be concerned about who knows the most about somebody's body, somebody better be able to change and feed.

BEV. After four kids you should be an expert.

LESTER. That's what I'm telling him.

ALEX. What Bev is saying is that you are irresponsible; four children from four different women.

LESTER. Hey, Alex! I can afford 'em, OK.

ALEX. Aw, man—

DIANE. Both of y'all need to stop. Come on, all this food I got here—sweet potato pie, pound cake, apple pie, triple double chocolate cake, peach cobbler—

(ALEX sneaks a piece of fried chicken.)

BEV. Hey, put that back. Put that back. Would you look at this! I knew he couldn't take it but so long.

ALEX *(still eating)*. Oh, this is good chicken. Now if y'all really want this reunion to go on without any more arguments, please don't tell Freida.

LESTER. See how hypocritical you are.

ALEX. He just called me hypocritical for eating a piece of
bird.

LESTER. You called me a sellout!

ALEX. That's beside the point, you are!

LESTER. And you are hypocritical.

ALEX. Y'all hear him.

LESTER. Put the chicken down then.

*(ALEX stands looking at LESTER with the chicken in his
hand.)*

BEV. Let that man eat some chicken. Y'all know white
women don't know how to feed a black man. That's
why he lost all that weight. Look at him.

DIANE. Leave Alex and Freida alone. Y'all go down to
the lake. Alex, catch some food for your wife. That's
why she blowing things up. The girl is hungry! But I'm
going to tell you now, I'm frying my fish. If she wants
to eat it fresh out the water that's her business. Kirk got
the fishing poles in that big bag over there.

BEV. I'm going to get me another piece of sweet potato
pie!

LESTER. Better watch it, Bev.

BEV. You better watch it. Looking at my behind.

DIANE. Hey, Alex, does she eat the scales and all?

BEV. It's called sushi, Dee.

DIANE. I know what it's called. I thought maybe she was
eating the scales and all, like in that movie with Tom
Hanks, with the mermaid—

ALEX. *Splash*! All right, that's enough, Dee.

BEV. Go ahead, Alex, taking up for his—woman.

ALEX. You two better be glad I know you.

LESTER *(pulls out a gun from the bag)*. What's he doing with this?

DIANE. I told Kirk to leave that thing in the house. No matter where we go he got to carry that thing.

LESTER *(points the gun)*. Maybe I should shoot the fish.

BEV. That's if you didn't scare them off.

LESTER. Freida and Loita are just having a good time, Bev.

BEV. Whatever.

(LESTER puts the gun back in the bag. ALEX gets another piece of chicken. They start to leave.)

LESTER. Hypocrite.

ALEX. Sellout. *(They exit arguing.)*

BEV. Go on with y'all white things. Make me sick.

DIANE. I don't know. To each his own.

BEV. To each his— Diane, what's wrong with this picture. The two that are the most successful, what they got?

DIANE. I know Alex, and I know Lester and I just don't believe they with those women because they—they—

BEV. It ain't a curse word, Dee, white. Say it. White.

DIANE. White.

BEV. You look at some of the brothers out here, especially those with a little education and money: Charles Barkley, Herschel Walker, that damn O.J. makes me wonder.

DIANE. Not our boys.

BEV. Humph, and then you got Chuck, not a white woman, but a white—

DIANE. Speaking of Chuck, I wonder what happened to him and Percy?

BEV. One thing, Alex and Lester better off than Chuck—

DIANE. Girl!

BEV. But they all better off than Sal, that's for sure. *(She takes a towel and swats bugs away.)*

DIANE. What I know is, God will work things out.

BEV. Easy for you to talk.

DIANE. What?

BEV. You got Kirk

DIANE. Kirk have his moments too. I couldn't stand to be around him when he decided to leave the army.

BEV. I don't believe after all those years they wouldn't give him that promotion.

DIANE. They had white officers with half of his experience being promoted to captain.

BEV. People talk about how things have changed. Just the same shit in a gold pot. Same thing at John Jay. When I'm around white people, I am serious as cancer. You can't afford to let up for a second, and even then it really doesn't matter because they are going to come after you no matter what.

DIANE. I know what you saying. He wanted that promotion so bad, Bev. I have seen Kirk angry, but I never saw Kirk get down. He was so hurt. They said he didn't finish in the top eighty percentile on that test.

BEV. What about when he pulled all those people out of that bunker in Lebanon?

DIANE. That's exactly what he asked them. They said that don't count. And Kirk scored really high on that last test too, but they said a lot of people scored higher. They put Colin Powell up in the front to make everybody think things have changed in the military, that's all.

BEV. Y'all gonna be all right?

DIANE. Oh, yeah. You know me and Kirk can pinch a
    penny. Kirk is thinking about opening a restaurant. You
    know that's always been my dream. I think we gonna do
    it.

BEV. Girl, with your recipes, humph. *(BEV becomes vis-
    ibly upset.)*

DIANE. What's wrong with you?

BEV. Nothing. I think about you and Kirk, Alex. Lester,
    Chuck, all black. All from Harlem. Makes me a little
    misty-eyed, that's all.

DIANE. Sal lost a child, Bev.

BEV. Sal was sick before that bastard shot— I was right in
    the house.

DIANE. I know.

BEV. Who got blamed for it? "You should have had him
    in the house." How you gonna keep a fifteen-year-old in
    the house these days?

DIANE. We didn't even stay in the house.

BEV. He wasn't the one that had to go down to the morgue
    and see our son with a hole in the back of his head.

DIANE. I know.

BEV. All he's been doing is punishing me ever since. Been
    stop sleeping with me. I knew Sal was cheating all
    along, but then he started putting it right in my face.

DIANE. What?

BEV. I thought they would have to put me in Bellevue,
    Ward 13, with all the loonies.

DIANE. You should have called me, Bev. Shoot.

BEV. And tell you what?

DIANE. Bev, you know I'm always here for you.

BEV. You don't know the half of it.

DIANE. Bev, you could call me anytime, you know that.

BEV. Used to be on the phone with you every day—

DIANE. Sometimes twice—three times a day.

BEV. Then once a week, once a month, once— I know you are busy but nobody is as busy as me—

DIANE. Bev, you know I would have stopped everything I was doing to—

BEV. Nobody is as busy as me.

DIANE. I didn't say I was as busy as you.

BEV. Ever since you gave yourself to God, you just stop calling. And when I call, I feel I got to watch what I say.

DIANE. I don't know why?

BEV. Neither do I.

DIANE. Bev, I got the kids, we been busy with the house, and Kirk, you know sometimes he's just another kid—

BEV. There you go—

DIANE. I'm sorry, Bev, I never realized—

BEV. That you are just a little above it all.

DIANE. No, Bev. You can tell me anything, Bev, you know that.

BEV *(pause)*. Sometimes, I just want to scream, but who in the hell is going to hear me?

DIANE. You want to talk about it now?

BEV. No, I'm fine. *(Pause.)* I just did some things I'm not too proud of.

DIANE. I know you were hurting, Bev.

BEV. Were? Hurting's not the word. I'm telling you, sometimes I still want them to put me in the grave with Julius.

DIANE. You need to stop talking like that.

BEV. Sal don't make it easier. One night one of Sal's women called me at my house and told me she was

sleeping with Sal, so I might as well leave him alone
because he didn't want me anyway.

DIANE. What?

BEV. I told that bitch. I said, look, bitch, you can have his
old rusty butt but if you ever call me at my house again
I'm gonna track your hoe ass down, and when I'm finish
with you, he won't want yo stink behind, and neither
will any other man. Then I started sleeping around like
some slut. I figured if he could do it so could I. Shoot,
I'm still young and fine and love me some— It's OK for
them to do it, but once a woman sleeps around, you are
in the slut-of-the-month club.

DIANE. That sleeping around, Bev—

BEV. See, Dee, there you go passing judgment. That's
what I don't need.

DIANE. I'm not passing judgment.

BEV. No matter how much religion you get, don't forget, I
knew you when you was in bobby socks and pigtails.

DIANE. I'm just concerned. It's dangerous, girl.

BEV. Well I stop giving up my ass, all right. Best thing to
happen to me was getting into law school. I want to
make sure that the next cop that kills some black kid
doesn't get off Scot-free. The only reason I stay with Sal
is because I don't have to worry about finances while
I'm in school. I know that sounds cold, but I put my
fifteen years in. Sal is like a scab from an old wound.
I'm just waiting for it to fall off.

DIANE. He still playing around?

BEV. I don't know and I don't care. I can't figure out who
would want to put up with his drunk butt anyway. Since
Julius died, all he does is work, come home, go up on
the avenue to Smalls Paradise. When he is home, he's

passed out, with the TV watching him. The only time I see a little life in him is when Kirk calls.

DIANE. I don't know what I would do if Kirk ever, ohh, get that thought out of my mind.

(Another ash can goes off.)

DIANE. What in the world?

BEV. Those are two nuts.

DIANE. Lord, what Lester see in her?

BEV. I don't know what he sees in her, but I know what she sees in him.

DIANE. Stop talking like that. Lester is like a brother.

BEV. Humph.

DIANE. Bev, what are you talking about?

BEV. What? Nothing.

DIANE. Bev, when you get that devilish look in your eye, I know it's something. What?

BEV. Nothing. I ever tell you about the time—

DIANE. I don't want to hear about it.

BEV. You just said—

DIANE. What?

BEV. We was eighteen years old, Dee.

DIANE. I told you I don't want to know about it. All these years. Kirk know? *(No answer.)* Bev!

BEV. He was great, Dee.

DIANE. I don't want to hear about it. Wait till I see Kirk.

BEV. The man whose aim is to please.

DIANE. Shut up!

BEV. It doesn't mean anything, it's just a good memory.

DIANE. Well keep it that way.

BEV. A good memory.

DIANE. Shussh!

(FREIDA and LOITA enter from the woods.)

LOITA. Hi. Did you hear us out there?

BEV. I know it's the Fourth of July but do y'all really have to blow everything up?

LOITA. Isn't that the purpose of the Fourth of July here in America?

BEV. Oh, that's right, you from France. That's a real accent?

LOITA *(in French)*. You wouldn't know a real accent from a fake accent if you heard it, so why are you asking?

BEV. Well excuse me.

LOITA. It is authentic. I was born in Paris.

FREIDA. Loita told me to think of all the people in my life that I didn't like. Then put them in a box and blow them up. I have a long list of politicians I'd like to blow up.

LOITA. It excites me to blow things up. I think of all the people who pissed me off, and there will always be someone who pisses you off. Even if you are having a, how you say, marvelously fabulous day. It is good to confront these people right away but sometimes it isn't possible, so you must carry the, how you say—

FREIDA. Unresolved stress—

LOITA. Yes, that is it, the unresolved stress with you. It is very unhealthy.

FREIDA. That must explain these headaches I get.

DIANE. Try eating a Big Mac!

FREIDA. I prefer the headaches.

BEV. So all this blowing shit up is about stress. Maybe if I—never work.

FREIDA. It works for me.

BEV. Well, it works for you, honey, go ahead. I need a nuclear bomb to take care of all my problems.

DIANE. Y'all need to go further into the woods with that mess though.

FREIDA. I know it sounds crazy but it's therapeutic. I have a lot of unresolved stress. Between dealing with the corrupt policies of this country, death penalty, foreign affairs, academia, people who won't understand the relationship I have with Alex, it goes on and on.

BEV. You should be used to it by now—

FREIDA. You would think that, but I'm not. I've dated black men before, but no one like Alex Earle. In fact, when we were blowing people up, the first person that came to my mind was this Indian cab driver in New York, October 1993. I was teaching at N.Y.U.

DIANE. What do you teach?

FREIDA (says it real fast). The social and political dynamics of interracial relationships.

LOITA. And she is a graphic artist. I think this is so wonderful.

FREIDA. Alex is waiting, at the corner, because no cab is going to pick up a black man downtown. I hail the cab. He stops and Alex gets in. So this cab driver speaks like no English. I tell him we're going to Harlem. He says, "No, no, I no go there, bad place. Very bad place."

DIANE. Lord! We know that story.

FREIDA. Alex didn't say a word. He just looked straight ahead. I said I'm not getting out of this cab. He looks at me and as sincerely as possible says, "Bad place, very bad place. Bad people. No you. You no bad people. The Harlem, bad people." I saw red! You are bad people, I told him. Why don't you get out of this country. You are not even a citizen, and you have the nerve to treat people second class. And you probably call yourself a Moslem.

BEV. No, you didn't.

FREIDA. Yes, I did.

DIANE. What happened?

FREIDA. I think the Moslem line got him. He leaps out of the cab and starts screaming, "Don't you talk to me about Allah, you are only a woman, don't you talk to me about Allah!" He made me so mad, I hit him over the head with my pocketbook, two or three good times, then the police arrived.

DIANE. What happened?

FREIDA. Normally, a white woman in distress, the only thing that stands a chance is a white male, but when I told them that Alex was an African-American history professor, that was it. They hauled us off in a police car.

DIANE. Alex, too?

FREIDA. That's why they did it. I contested the damn thing. The judge even said I should expect to meet resistance about taking a yellow medallion to Harlem, City College or no City College. My own attorney urged me to leave it alone. She said it's OK to be interested in the myth, but don't take it too far.

BEV. If I was your attorney, I would have taken everybody to court, and then to the bank.

FREIDA. She *was* a friend of mind. That was my first date with Alex! It hasn't gotten any better. So you see the stress builds every day. Every time I catch a cab in New York I think about that cab driver.

LOITA. The race thing. I don't understand this race thing in America.

BEV. As if they don't have race problems in France.

LOITA. Yes, but when you are French you are French, it doesn't matter the color.

BEV. Honey, that is some bullshit, and let me tell you if you walk down 125th Street with Lester you will find out real quick about the race problem in America because the sister will have your ass.

DIANE. Bev!

BEV. They will!

LOITA. Why, I don't understand—

BEV. Well let me spell it out for you.

DIANE. Bev!

BEV. All the sisters are going to know that the French-bomb model is with Lester McMichael because of who he is. And they know you wouldn't have given him the time of day if he was just another brother from the hood.

LOITA. Is that what the sisters from Harlem would think?

BEV. No, sweetheart, that's what the sisters from Harlem would know.

LOITA. And you are a sister from Harlem, yes?

BEV. Born and raised, sweetheart.

LOITA. So you have these feelings about Lester and I? Hmm?

BEV. Let me tell you something, sweetheart—

DIANE. Bev, don't start.

BEV. No, I want to get sister girl straight—

DIANE. Jesus, Bev!

LOITA. No, please, I want to hear what the sister from Harlem has to say.

BEV. The problem is, y'all white hookers can't wait to get your hands on the cream of the crop. And that's literally and figuratively.

FREIDA. I really feel like defending that.

DIANE. Lord, let's not turn this into a race riot, OK?

LOITA. I did not even know who is this Lester Mc-Michael—

DIANE. Wait a minute. You didn't know who Lester Mc-Michael was?

BEV. Yeah, right.

DIANE. What planet are you living on? That's our Lester. Shoot!

FREIDA. Maybe you should tell them how you met Lester, Loita.

BEV. Yeah, I want to know. How did Lester end up with you?

LOITA. I was sitting in Cafe Lechamp, in Paris, when Lester came in with his entourage.

BEV. See, that's just what I'm talking about.

LOITA. I did not know who is this.

BEV. You didn't have to know. Black man, entourage!

LOITA. Whatever.

BEV. What did she say?

FREIDA. That was clever.

LOITA. He is staring across the cafe to me. And I am staring to him too. I like to stare to people. My psychiatrist tells me I am looking for my parents because I was an adoption child. But the psychiatrist, they tell everybody they are looking for the parents, or the, how you say, inner child.

DIANE. Who raised you, honey?

LOITA. I was raised by the sun. I blew up my parents a long time ago.

BEV. This chick is gone.

LOITA. He came to me, and said to me I was making him nervous. Many times I know I make the men nervous but this man is so strong and so powerful. I felt honored to make him nervous. He told me I, how you say, hypnotized him. He is a very charming man, and he is so—

BEV. Generous?

LOITA. Yes, generous, but I'm not speaking of money, I have lots of money.

(LOITA's next line should be continuous throughout BEV's line.)

BEV. Neither am I, and I don't have lots of money.

LOITA. And I am not a hooker. He is a special man.

BEV. I know what his specialty is.

LOITA. And you know what his specialty was and that is why I am with him?

BEV. You won't be for long, sweetheart, keep talking.

FREIDA. Hey she's young. How many of us would have passed up a chance to be with a superstar at twenty-two? *(FREIDA raises her own hand.)* Well maybe Bruce Springsteen, Jesse Jackson or Huey P. Newton.

BEV. Hmmm.

LOITA. Lester and I have a soulship. That is what he calls it. A soulship.

BEV. Lester ran that line on you, too.

LOITA. But it is true. No matter what happens we will always be a part of each other. He never is concerned about what man or what woman is in my life and he can be with whatever woman he chooses, it doesn't bother me because no matter what happens we will always be a part of each other. All these worries men and women have about who is with this person and who is with that person to me is so, how you say—petty.

BEV. Did she just call me petty?

FREIDA. I think she meant it euphemistically.

LOITA. When you think of the whole universe, with all the suns, all the planets, with all the aliens, everything else is so—petty. And no one lives so long.

(BEV and DIANE look at LOITA as if she is crazy.)

FREIDA. Makes sense to me. You have to admit, a lot of women spend too much time worrying about the petty things, as she calls it.

BEV *(starts to walk away)*. I have been through too much real shit to listen to this. Petty, aliens, kiss my black—

FREIDA. But think about it. Everything most of us do, is with a man in mind. How we dress, how we eat, how we look. How we get along with each other. Most women can't even get along because they have men on the brain.

(BEV stops to listen.)

Look, I am not one of those women who has taken feminism to an extreme, hold the door for me please. But some of our attitudes need to be checked. It begins with how we see ourselves.

DIANE. Thank God somebody makes sense.

FREIDA. Just don't oppress me, don't abuse me, don't put labels on me, give me equal pay for the work I do and don't think I'm supposed to jump through hoops because I'm a woman and you're a man, white, black, green or polka dot.

BEV. Now, I heard that—

FREIDA. And I am not going to make any excuse for my intelligence or my femininity. I know I'm going to repulse some and attract others. Those that are repulsed can take a long ride on the N train to Nowhere as far as I'm concerned.

BEV. I'm surprised Alex wasn't on that N train.

FREIDA. Exactly my point. Alex, we all know, is a proud black man, and I love him for that. I have to figure OK, we have to make this work. I listen to him talk about the sins of the white race everyday. But can I blame him? Any blind person can turn on their TV and see the problem. Not to mention the black holocaust, the annihilation of the native Americans, genocide in the inner city, it's non-stop. And I cannot as a citizen of this country turn my back or close my eyes to the facts, like most people I know. So what do I do? I just try to be the best "woman" I can be, but for me first—

LOITA & BEV. Intelligence and femininity.

BEV. I like that, Freida.

FREIDA. I don't agree with everything that comes out of the mouth of Alex Earle, believe me, and when I think he's wrong I try to make him see it. But sometimes he walks in our house after a long day and I can see the weight of the whole world on his shoulders, that's when I lay him down and try to bathe, massage, and love some of that weight off. Once he's in that house I'm his woman and he is my man, and that's it.

DIANE. Now see, there ain't nothing wrong with that. The Bible says, honor thy husband.

BEV. She's not talking about honoring nobody, Dee. The Bible's the one got us in this fix in the first place.

FREIDA. That's not exactly what I meant, Diane, but if it works for you—hey, can't knock those family values.

DIANE. It was good enough for my mother, and her mother, and believe me they took more from their husbands than I ever take from Kirk.

BEV. Y'all got all the answers. Where in the hell did I go wrong?

DIANE *(hugs BEV)*. Stop blaming yourself! You know it's got nothing to do with you.

FREIDA. I know it's not my place to say this, but given everything I heard, Ms. John Jay Law School, you are doing better than I would under the circumstances.

(BEV gives FREIDA a hug. Then to LOITA.)

And you, whether anyone wants to admit it or not, are living a lot of our dreams—and fears.

(They all look at LOITA. FREIDA gives LOITA a hug. LOITA hugs BEV. The hug is not returned. LOITA goes to hug DIANE. DIANE extends her hand. They shake hands.)

DIANE. Well at least Loita don't have to worry about washing nasty three-day-old socks, uggh. Gets on my last nerve.

(KIRK, LESTER and ALEX enter.)

KIRK. What y'all yapping about?

DIANE. Yapping? I was telling them about your three-day-old socks.

KIRK. Because you don't do the laundry on time.

BEV. Where's Sal?

KIRK. Sitting in the car. He'll be here in a minute.

BEV. Oh God.

KIRK. What can I do if Dee don't do the laundry on time.

FREIDA. Alex puts his socks through the smell test. If he can stand the smell then he can wear the socks.

ALEX. Freida—

DIANE. Kirk ain't satisfied unless the socks can stand up and walk by themselves.

LESTER. Damn Kirk.

KIRK. Well, do the laundry on time then.

FREIDA. I had to buy Alex new socks just for this trip.

BEV. Oh, then those not your feet I'm smelling, Alex. Must be some dog pooh around here. Unless they Kirk's.

(They all laugh.)

KIRK. My feet smell sweet.

BEV. Men! Girl, let me tell you, I went to visit my daddy earlier this year, and when I came back home, Sal had tried to cook. Lord have mercy. Grease this thick was in the frying pan. He never changed the grease. Crumbs were all over the kitchen and the roaches was going hut, two, three, four. Soon as he gets here he's going to try to barbecue like Eddie Murphy's uncle. "Now that's a fire!"

KIRK. I got news for you, me and Sal, can barbecue!
Speaking of. *(He prepares some food.)*

ALEX. A man's place ain't in the kitchen.

LESTER. As much as you like to eat. My father taught me
that a man ain't a man unless he can cook.

ALEX. Men need to be able to cook for survival but—but
leave home economics where it belongs.

FREIDA. And where's that, Alex?

ALEX. Hmm. Why every time I say something it kinda
comes out wrong.

LESTER. Maybe you shouldn't say nothing?

FREIDA. Alex, why are you trying to give everybody a
warped vision of our marriage?

LESTER. Why you fronting, Alex?

ALEX. All right, all right, I cook every now and then,
'cause if I didn't, I might starve. It's a matter of survival.

FREIDA. I have no problem cooking for my man but most
times I'm just as busy as Alex. Mr. McMichael, do you
do everything perfectly?

LOITA. No, he never puts the cap on the toothpaste and he
never puts the seat up before he pees.

KIRK & LESTER. I always put the seat up!

DIANE. Uggh. Nothing worse than sitting in pee!

FREIDA. Unless it's waking up in a puddle of drool.

EVERYBODY. UGGH.

ALEX. You drool, too!

FREIDA. We are not talking about me. We are talking
about you, bow-wow-ruff-ruff, yippy, ki-yi-oh!

BEV. Only thing worse is kudda berry draws.

THE MEN. That ain't me!

LESTER. Fellas, we walked in on a Oprah Winfrey session. We are not going to win.

BEV. Call it what you want. But y'all just think we should be there to wait on y'all whenever y'all call: food call, sanitation call, mail call, bootie call.

FREIDA. That's what I don't need. What I do need is to know that if I cook, or clean, or give excellent sex, that it's appreciated.

BEV. And reciprocated.

DIANE & FREIDA. Right!

KIRK. I don't care what y'all say I don't wear kudda berry draws.

BEV. Come on, Kirk, let's see those socks walk by themselves. Hut, two, three, four. Hut, two, three, four. (She tries to pull KIRK's socks off. KIRK runs.)

KIRK. Better leave me alone.

DIANE. Lord, I haven't laughed this hard since—

KIRK. Admit it, Dee, since we was the Bow-Wow Club.

DIANE. All right, Kirk. Since you have to be right.

BEV. Lester, sing "Funky Melody" before Kirk starts barbecuing.

LESTER. Oh—naw.

EVERYBODY. Come on, Lester.

(As LESTER prepares to sing, CHUCK and PERRY enter.)

LESTER. Hey, what you guys got lost?

CHUCK. How can anybody find this place?

PERRY. Kirk you said get off at exit 64, right? That's halfway through Virginia.

DIANE. Y'all get something to eat and drink, and relax, Lester was just getting ready to sing.

PERRY. "Funky Melody," please. I'd die for "Funky Melody." Please.

LESTER. You don't have to die for "Funky Melody."

DIANE. Lord, Lester, sing before this man dies, we sure don't want that on our conscience.

(LESTER sings. As he does LOITA dances around him.)

LESTER.

It was the night of the funky melody
It was the night of a groovy sound
It was the night of the funky melody
When people from all around,
got funky
with the groovy sound

It was in the air
People from everywhere
Were affected by the jam.
The stars turned black
As the mystery attacked
Affecting the world
With this groovy sound.

(Everyone joins in and starts to dance.)

It was the night of the funky melody.
It was the night of the groovy sound
It was the night of the funky melody

(SAL enters. He has a bottle in his hand. He is stumble drunk. He sings with LESTER. Loud and off-key.)

SAL.

It was the night of the funky melody.
It was the night of a groovy sound!

(He hugs LESTER.)

Sorry, Les!

(He continues to sing, hugging LESTER.)

SAL. Look, I'm singing with Lester! It's all right, right, Kirk?

KIRK. Yeah, man.

SAL. Right?

KIRK. Yeah, Sal!

SAL. Because we the Bow-Wow Club, right, Alex?

ALEX. Right on, brother.

SAL. Lester is the man!

LESTER. If you say so, Sal. But everybody knows you're the man. You Sal.

(Everything stops. A long pause as SAL looks at CHUCK. SAL can barely stand up. KIRK holds him.)

KIRK. Come on, why don't you lie down under the tree, Sal.

SAL. Hey, Chuck, I ain't mad at ya. *(Sings.)* "I ain't mad at ya. I ain't mad at ya." You ever meet that little Tupac motherfucker, Lester?

LESTER. Yeah.

SAL. "I ain't mad at ya." One thing I want to know, Chuck. Now I ain't mad at ya. Who's the man, and who's the girl? Please tell me you the man, Chuck.

CHUCK. Sal, there are not enough words in the history of language to describe human sexuality.

SAL. Oh, now you a homointellectual.

EVERYBODY. Sal—

SAL. Let's finish singing, everybody! *(Sings.)* "It was the night of the funky melody." I woulda been a star too. Right, Kirk? Blood sweat and motherfucking tears! Tell them what my forty time was, Kirk.

KIRK. 4.4.

SAL. Hear that! 4.4! Can't tell these young boys shit today! I woulda bust they ass. I woulda been saying, "Show me the money!" Young boys be laughing at me when I tell them about my glory days! Call me a has-been. Legend in my own mind. They just don't know, right, Kirk?

KIRK. Right, man.

BEV. Why don't you listen to Kirk and go lay down.

SAL. But you know what? I don't give a damn. I could care less than a good goddamn. Sorry, Dee. Hey, Chuck, I cursed. I apologize, Reverend. Oh that's right, you not a reverend no more. What the hell are you now besides a—I'm sorry, I won't say it.

CHUCK. Sal, I know you are drunk but that's enough. Jesus!

SAL. Oops. I changed my mind. Kiss my ass, you fairy motherfucker. Did you hear what I said? *(He stumbles around looking for a beer. He sees the football. He picks it up.)* Hey, Kirk!

KIRK. What! What!

SAL. Hut one, hut two.

BEV. Sal, stop.

SAL. We playing football, Bev! Why you always on my back?

BEV. Put it down, Sal!

SAL. Throw me a pass, Kirk. One for the Sal-onse!

BEV. Sal!

KIRK. One pass. One pass, Bev.

SAL. All right, you got to call it out—

KIRK (*as a quarterback*). Team down. Ready, set—

SAL. On three, on three.

KIRK. Team down.

SAL. Guard me, Alex.

ALEX. Come on, man.

KIRK (*losing his temper*). Guard him, Alex!!

(ALEX acts like he's guarding SAL.)

KIRK. Team down, ready, set, hut one, hut two, hut three.

(KIRK drops back and passes the ball to SAL. He catches it but falls hard on the ground. KIRK, ALEX and LESTER run over to him.)

SAL. Y'all see that shit. Yall see that. (*He gets up and tries to do a touchdown dance but falls again.*)

BEV. OK, Sal, enough is enough. I'm not angry anymore. I am beyond angry, pissed off, or livid! I am hurt, I am embarrassed and I am very sad. So I'm going to drive us home. You can yell, and scream all you want in the car. Kirk, drive us back to your house so I can get my car.

SAL. Bev—
BEV. What!?
SAL. I'm fucked up.
BEV. I know.
SAL. Fucked usspssh!
BEV. No, Sal.

(SAL throws up and passes out. PERRY walks off.)

BEV. Oh, Sal.
LESTER. What now? Want me to throw some water on his
   face. Wake his ass up.
BEV *(cleaning SAL off)*. No. Just leave him right where he
   is. Let him sleep it off, otherwise he'll get up and it will
   be worse. I am so tired of this!
KIRK. Damn. Take the Bow—outta Bow-Wow. Shiooot.
   Shit yeah I said shit, Dee. Shit damn shit!

*(CHUCK notices that PERRY has walked off. He runs
off to find him.)*

SCENE TWO

*(Lights up on PERRY sitting in the woods. As CHUCK
approaches, he stands up.)*

CHUCK. Perry.
PERRY. I fucking lost. Which way is the car?
CHUCK. Perry—
PERRY. I don't care what you say I am not staying here
   with these Neanderthals. If you want to stay, fine, but I

am going home. Because when that jackass wakes up again, and begins to insult me again, I don't care how big he is, or how tough he is, I am going to bite his balls off. So to save myself that embarrassment, and the sight and taste of blood and gore, I'm going home.

CHUCK. I'm sorry.

PERRY. Yes, you are, because if you don't see that this is pointless then you are sorry, and I feel sorry for you.

CHUCK. You don't get it, do you?

PERRY. No, I don't, and no matter what you say I don't believe you do, either.

CHUCK. Perry—

PERRY. If you want to stick around and be insulted go ahead. Personally I grew out of the sadomasochist phase a long time ago.

CHUCK. Point taken.

PERRY. Grown men acting like little boys. I'm not into little boys! This isn't easy for me you know. Not only do I have to watch you get eaten by these hyenas, but I have to protect my own ass because you are so wrapped up in this reunion that you are incapable of coming to my defense or your own.

CHUCK. It's just Sal and he's drunk, don't you—

PERRY. No, it isn't! It's all of them. Every last one of them, except miss hot-and-trot-chickadee, and the herb woman, the no meat-eater, Freida.

CHUCK. Perry, it's a shock to them. It's my fault. I should have warned them. I just felt it would be better face to face. I was wrong.

PERRY. Now you want to play the victim. Chuck, it's not your fault. You should be mad as hell! I'm worried about how calmly you are taking all of this.

CHUCK. It's hard, Perry.

PERRY. I wish we were talking sex here but unfortunately we are not. I am going to drive to D.C., and catch up with my mom. I need a little nurturing. I'll take her to see the fireworks. I'll probably stop by the shop, and check on Lenny. You know how manic he gets with crowds.

CHUCK. You want me to go with you?

PERRY. No. You need this. Why, I don't know, but if you are not ready to leave after that, then you need to stay and find whatever it is you are looking for, but I can't help you. I can't. Which way is the car?

CHUCK. See how much I care about you. If I woulda left you out here you would have been lost in the woods.

PERRY. And I love you very much too. Which way is the car? *(They exit.)*

SCENE THREE

(An hour later. It is dusk. Lights come up on DIANE, BEV, ALEX and FREIDA. SAL is still passed out. DI-ANE and BEV are preparing to leave. They are packing to go back to the house. KIRK enters.)

DIANE. Did you see them?

KIRK. Naw. I went down to the parking lot. The car is still there but no sign of them. I walked over by the lake—no sign of them.

ALEX. That's it for the Bow-Wow Club.

KIRK. I'll always be a Bow-Wow. You don't want to be a Bow-Wow, that's your business. Me, I'm Bow-Wow.

DIANE. Let's take this stuff down to the car.

KIRK. You want to go home, go home. Go! I'm going to wait for Chuck to come back and I'm waiting for Sal to wake up. We gonna have a little talk.

BEV. I doubt if Chuck comes back. Would you come back if you had that waiting for you?

KIRK. Y'all go. I'll stay until Sal gets up. Meet you back at the house.

(The sound of lovemaking is heard, loud and intense. Everyone stops in their tracks and listens. The sounds increase in intensity.)

KIRK *(howls)*. LESTER-ONSE!

DIANE. That's Lester and that girl?

KIRK. Well it ain't Sal and Bev. Damn sure ain't me and you.

(They all listen to the sounds of the lovemaking. As it intensifies.)

ALEX. Where's it coming from?

KIRK. Sounds like right over there.

ALEX. I feel like peeping just like y'all did to me twenty years ago.

KIRK. You want to?

DIANE & FREIDA. Kirk. Alex—

ALEX. Just a thought, Dee.

(The sounds intensify then subsides.)

DIANE. Out in public!

KIRK. Lester-onse!

BEV. Shut up, Kirk.

FREIDA. Oh my God.

KIRK. Sound like us last night, Dee.

DIANE. You better stop that lying, because I don't scream like that. You ain't never heard me scream like that. In fact I don't even scream.

KIRK. That's why the neighbors called the police, woulda thought somebody was killing you.

DIANE. Bev, would you talk to this man before I kill him.

KIRK. That's my baby, she's so refined.

DIANE. I'm gonna put a firecracker in your front pocket. Lets see how refined you think I am then.

KIRK. Oh, hurt me, baby!

(LOITA and LESTER enter from the woods. Both are fully dressed. LOITA's hair is disheveled. LESTER's shirt is buttoned unevenly. They look as if they have just finished making love. They are hugging. The group just stares at them. No one says a word.)

LESTER *(whispers)*. Why is everybody looking at us? Were we that loud?

ALEX & KIRK. No, not really.

DIANE & BEV. Yes!

LOITA. Ohhhhh.

ALEX. Hey, Lester. Some of us got it, some of us don't?

LOITA. Ohhhh.

(BEV looks at LOITA and rolls her eyes. She walks away.)

DIANE. Bev. You all right?

BEV. I'm fine.

LESTER. Where's everybody going?

(They all stop and look at LESTER.)

ALEX. You seem to be the only one having a good time.

KIRK. What about me? I'm having a great time. A scarribulous time!

FREIDA. Alex, why don't you stay here with Lester and Kirk just in case Chuck comes back. They may need your help with Sal. OK, honey?

ALEX. I don't want to— Somebody has got to walk with y'all to the car.

DIANE. We are not helpless. I learned a thing or two being married to an army officer. Don't look at me like that. Shooot. God protects those who protect themselves.

(The WOMEN start to leave. LOITA doesn't move.)

DIANE. Coming, sweetheart.

(LOITA gives LESTER a kiss and walks away with the WOMEN.)

KIRK. Lester-onse! *(Hugs LESTER and kisses him on the cheek.)* See, Lester still Bow-Wow to the core.

LESTER. She's just got this thing about doing it in public.

KIRK. Kiss my bootie. In public?

ALEX. Nobody wants to kiss your bootie in public, Kirk.

LESTER. I can't get her to understand. I'm a public figure. All I need is a front page in *The New York Post.* "Lester

McMichael caught in Central Park with his pants down
with French supermodel Loita."

KIRK. My man! Lester-onse!

ALEX. Grow up!

KIRK. Ease up, Alex. We are just having some fun.

ALEX. What do you see in her besides the obvious?

LESTER. Is there anything else?

ALEX. Maybe a ladder. You should be ashamed of yourself calling that girl your woman.

LESTER. She's more woman than you ever had.

ALEX. Oh, here we go. Man-o-a-man-o. Back on Lenox
Ave. with the hustlers and pimps. I left that shit a long
time ago, Lester. I hoped you had too. But you still playing the McDaddy role. Well at least get a woman that
represents you. Then again maybe she does.

LESTER. Oh, because Freida has got all these fucking de-
grees and shit, I guess that makes her the perfect excuse
for you.

ALEX. You would never understand, man. Too shallow—

LESTER. Shallow? Stop hiding behind a bunch of letters
and then come and talk to me about shallow.

KIRK (howls). Forget all that! Lester, what I want to know
is—and tell me if I'm outta line, Lester—does she give
good buzzard?

ALEX. Aw, man!

KIRK. I said for Lester to tell me if I was outta line.

ALEX. I'll tell you. You are outta line.

KIRK. What happen to you, Alex-onse?

ALEX. Don't Alex-onse me. I think I respect women more
than that, even if they are—

KIRK. So she likes an audience, Lester?

(CHUCK enters.)

EVERYBODY. Where in the hell have you been?

CHUCK. Perry went home and then I just walked around for a while. I had some thinking to do. Look, I really need to talk—

KIRK. We were worried about you, man.

CHUCK. I see you are all looking real hard. I got something to say to y'all—

KIRK *(rubbing his hands together).* Wait a minute. Lester was just going to tell us about Loita's buzzard.

ALEX. Leave it alone, man.

KIRK. I wanna know.

CHUCK. Loita's buzz— May I say something?

LESTER. OK, time out. Time out! Chuck, just a minute. I am going to answer this question this time, only because this is supposed to be a Bow-Wow reunion. All right. All right?

CHUCK. I'm trying to say something.

KIRK. Just a minute, Chuck. Bow-Wow time!

(It is suggested that during this section LESTER plays the comic element of the scene in the form of Richard Pryor, Eddie Murphy, Bill Cosby or Redd Foxx.)

LESTER. I have had women from the four corners of the earth, all kinds of girls, white, yellow, red, brown and beautiful black pearls. Old and young, smooth and wrinkled, fat and skinny

KIRK *(laughs).* Oh, shit. Fat and skinny. Y'all remember that saying? Fat and skinny went to bed, fat made a fart and skinny dropped dead?

ALEX & LESTER. Yeah.

KIRK. Nothing. I just wanted to know if y'all remembered it, that's all. Go ahead.

LESTER *(pause)*. Like I was saying. So tall, I had to climb a ladder. That's for you, Alex. Fucked little short vision of beauty, heard their hearts go pitter-patter. Pussy so tight, lubrication couldn't get me in. Pussy just right, just wanna roll all night. Pussy so wide, I could walk inside and hide. But the buzzard is still the prerequisite for all a good lay. It's the ultimate foreplay.

(During this section, LESTER demonstrates as he says his speech. KIRK get completely lost in LESTER's descriptions. ALEX does too, but tries to hide it. CHUCK has other things on his mind, also, but they are not as obvious. There may be vocal response to LESTER.)

LESTER. You got the slow rollers, roll the head around like this. Make me scream like a—bitch. But I love to float in a deep throat. You got those that just like to nibble, but who am I to quibble, make my head roll like Sybil. Some have sharp teeth, I keep them away from my meat. I like those that do it with suction before we start fucking. The fabulous suction actions! Hmm. Get it. Get it, baby. Then there are those that like to lick it like a lollipop, 'Juicy Fruit, Tootsie Roll, please don't stop. Put it to the test, here's the best, those that slobber, feels so good with the glorious slobber gobbers. But, cousins, never have I had anyone buzzin on my gluzzin, and I ain't fussin, though she makes me do some cussin. Shit! while she's sucking on the gluzzin, no one can beat her, and that's my Loita.

KIRK. I knew it! I knew It! I could look at her lips and tell.

CHUCK. You could what?

ALEX. You got a lot of nerve, man.

KIRK. What category you put her in?

ALEX. Lester, if you answer that, I am going to punch you in your face, man. I'm not lying.

CHUCK. This is sick. I'm going to be sick.

KIRK. What about Freida?

ALEX. What? Don't go there, Kirk.

LESTER. So Freida got you hooked, man. You don't mess around anymore?

ALEX. Man—

KIRK. Well—

ALEX. Doesn't marriage mean anything to y'all? I am married. The only reason you asked me and Lester those ridiculous questions, is because Freida is white and Loita is—aw, come on, man, I am not stupid enough to answer you. How would you like it if I asked you how Dee gives head?

KIRK. Go on.

CHUCK. I swear you guys are making me sick with this.

ALEX. Forget about it.

KIRK. Ask me.

ALEX. No.

KIRK. Dee don't do the buzzard.

LESTER & ALEX. What? No buzzard?

KIRK. That's what I said. Dee never once did the buzzard.

ALEX (holding back a laugh). Now that is sad, man.

LESTER. When is the last time you had a woman's mouth wrapped around your shaft doing magical wonders?

KIRK *(irritated)*. Dee just don't do the buzzard and that's that.

ALEX. When we were kids, sisters didn't give head, or at least they didn't admit to giving head, remember?

LESTER. And no brother would admit to giving head either.

ALEX. Do you give head, Kirk?

KIRK. Like Diane says, it's better to give than to receive.

LESTER. One time I had this woman who didn't believe black men gave head. By the time the night was over, she was screaming, "Get the hell outta there, please!"

ALEX. Wait a minute. Kirk, you were the first one of us to get married. You were what, twenty-two. So If you didn't get head before then that means you never got any, unless you fooled around on Dee.

CHUCK. You guys really should feel ashamed of yourselves.

ALEX. I know you are not passing judgment.

KIRK. What about Freida?

ALEX. Answer the question, Kirk!

KIRK. You first.

ALEX. No. Answer the question.

KIRK. After you.

ALEX. No, after you

KIRK. No, after you.

ALEX. I got to know. After all y'all put me through when I was a kid. Now I finally got a chance to have one on you. OK. Just to hear your answer. I love Freida. And I know y'all got a problem with that, too bad. I never cheated on her. And whether she gives a good buzzard or not is none of your business. But there was this one time, just before we got married. One of my ex-students seduced me in my office. It wasn't my fault. But talking about the buzzard. The best buzzard I ever had.

LESTER. One of your ex-students. How old was she?

ALEX. Don't worry about it. Kirk—

KIRK. I was stationed in Korea. This redneck from Texas took me to this place everybody was talking about.

LESTER. You got the Kum-che squat.

KIRK. I knew you would know about the squat, Lester! We go to this place. It's like a massage parlor, right. I had this fine-a-roonie. We drank some sake, she oiled me down, gave me a massage, and yes she did the buzzard, and then, I laid on my back and she gave me the squat. Aw, man. I was told that there are three types pussy in the world: good, better and best. But this was, man, if God made anything better than the squat, he saved it for hisself. Huckle my berry!

ALEX. All right. Let's change the subject. Here we are grown and black talking about sex like some degenerate perverts.

LESTER. For talking about pussy? I'm a man! I talk about pussy, all right.

CHUCK. You are talking about your mothers, you are talking about your sisters, aunts, daughters—

LESTER. Wait a minute, Chuck, you are going to tell me that when you see a fine woman you stop and think about your mother?

ALEX. Probably the only way he sees women nowadays.

CHUCK. I don't believe you just said that.

ALEX. I don't believe I said it myself. Fellas. We could be talking about interest rates at the Carver Bank, Jesse Jackson, Farrakan, The New South Africa, the Michael

Jordan phenomenon, anything but sex, like we are dis-
covering it for the first time.

KIRK. How often do we get a chance to just let loose like
this, Alex. It's just for old time's sake. I know I
wouldn't talk about this with anybody else. I'm going to
tell you, man, it's been years! And it feels good, Alex,
you know it.

ALEX *(after a moment)*. Since you put it that way. All
right. I have to confess. I think about sex all the time
too. I thought when I got older I wouldn't think about it
anymore. I'm into my work, and all I'm thinking about
is pussy. I pride myself on being a focused individual. I
got all these political agendas, trying to get our forty
acres, you know, but what's right behind the thought to
the racist I'm about to address? The ass of the woman
standing across the room. The shit bugs me. I think
something is wrong with me. I really think the problem
is that black men are innately polygamous. We weren't
meant to be with one woman. That's some European
concept from when they came out of them caves and
lived in those little villages. There is nothing I can do
about it. I'm in America, and most women don't, and
won't understand. I just come to accept that pussy will
be the constant companion of every thought in my life.
That was my secret. I didn't want to come back here and
admit that, because I honestly thought y'all were past
that. Damn it feels good to get that off my chest.

LESTER. I got to tell y'all, you guys really surprised me.
We took an oath when we formed the Bow-Wow Club
saying that we would be Bow-Wow to the day we died,
and now I'm the only one that's still trying to fuck every
fine woman in the world. And you know something, I

don't see nothing wrong with that. Either y'all crazy or I'm sick.

ALEX. You are sick, and so am I. Because as much as I hate to admit it, I'm still Bow-Wow. I may not act out on it like you but I'm still Bow-Wow.

KIRK. I don't know how you could give it up, Chuck?

CHUCK. Oh, I'm still Bow-Wow. Now I get the best of both worlds, I give and receive.

ALEX, LESTER & KIRK. Awww. Nawwww.

CHUCK. What shock you! That's what I have to do to receive some attention?

ALEX. You didn't have to tell us that!

CHUCK. Why?

KIRK. Because we don't want to think about it.

CHUCK. Because all of you have a huge problem dealing with the truth!

(The WOMEN enter from the woods.)

MEN. Oh, shit!

DIANE. Look around you, Kirk. Look at the fresh outdoors. Take a good look because this is your new home. Sleep out here like the dog you are, because if you come back to my house you better sleep with one eye open, Buster Buzzard!

KIRK. Dee. Dee. What did I say, Dee? Aw, snookum-ookum.

(DIANE punches KIRK in the stomach and leaves. KIRK turns and leaves doubled over. FREIDA walks to ALEX. BEV stands quietly.)

LESTER. How long y'all been listening?

CHUCK. Long enough, obviously.

FREIDA *(calmly)*. Alex, you know I hear them all the time. Colleagues, coeds, mothers, "Oh Professor Earle is so sexy, so fine," but I think to myself, my Alex would never do anything, he would never be that weak, irresponsible or—

ALEX. Freida—

FREIDA. Humm. I was wrong.

ALEX. Freida—

FREIDA *(snaps)*. Disgusting and unacceptable, Professor Alex Earle. A student.

ALEX. Baby— Freida, look. Baby— I swear— Baby, please.

(FREIDA just looks at ALEX and heads toward the woods. ALEX follows her. LOITA kisses LESTER passionately.)

LOITA. Hmmm. You like that?

LESTER. Yeah.

LOITA. Hmmmm. Lester, a buzzard is a nasty bird.

LESTER. See, it's not a bird thing, it's like a hmm thing, see, hmmmmm.

LOITA *(screams)*. I don't care! I like birds. I like cockatiels! I do a real good cockatiel. Wanna see. Right here. Right now! Line up Bow-Wow club! Let me demonstrate the cockatiel! And then I am going to fuck all of you dry, one by one. *(She sits on the picnic table and opens her mouth, taking off her clothes. LESTER puts her clothes back on.)*

LESTER. Loita!

(She gets down and runs off. BEV stops LESTER as SAL sits up unnoticed by the others. He listens then eventually lays down again.)

BEV. Lester you know I used to be just like her. After all these years, after all the records sold, world tours, interviews in exotic places, magazine covers, you still haven't changed. You still the same little boy who let Mike Martin smell your fingers after you were with me. My very first time. I knew I could never take you seriously. I knew that at fifteen years old. And you know what? I still can't. What a joke! *(She exits.)*

CHUCK. Les, you slept with Bev? Man oh man. What in the hell am I going to do with you guys? Y'all are disgusting.

(KIRK and ALEX enter.)

ALEX. I knew I should have kept my black ass home.

KIRK. I don't care what you say I ain't too proud to beg.

LESTER. Man, we really screwed up.

CHUCK. To think I used to be just like y'all.

ALEX. Not only did I let myself get conned into this little holiday embarrassment, now she is mad at me, about something she's not even supposed to know about.

KIRK. We got to get Sal up. I got to go see about Dee. Sal, you slept long enough. Get up!

(They all try and lift SAL.)

SAL. Damn! My freaking head. I had this dream. I think it was a dream. We were back in Harlem. Me and Alex were leaving Alex's apartment as usual. We stopped to pick up Lester but he wasn't home. When we got off the elevator Chuck and Kirk tried to stop me from going outside. Kirk, you kept saying don't go. The more you said it, the more I had to go. When I got out in front of the building the sun was shining and there were all these people cheering. On top of a red Eldorado was Lester and Bev, butt-naked, fucking. Ain't that some shit. *(A long silence.)* Where the women at?

ALEX. Kirk and Lester pissed them off.

KIRK. Me?

ALEX. It was your idea to have this damn reunion!

KIRK. Ain't nobody twist your arm and make you come!

ALEX. You called my house almost eight times—a day!

SAL. Lester, you ever fuck Bev?

LESTER. What?

SAL. You heard me. You ever fuck Bev? Tell me the truth, man.

LESTER *(pause)*. Sal, it was a long time before y'all—

SAL. I thought so.

LESTER. Sal, we were in high school. You and Bev didn't get tight until—

SAL. Don't tell me when me and Bev got tight! That's why you usta always tell me not to marry her. "Sal, you sure you know what you doing, man?"

LESTER. You had dreams, Sal. I thought all marriage was going to do was get in the way of your dreams.

SAL. I always wondered about that, but in my heart I knew. You could have told me you fucked my wife!

LESTER. It was a long time ago, Sal, I don't see why it's so important now.

SAL. It was important to me then, and it's important to me now! And both of y'all kept that shit a secret from me for all these years. What y'all think I couldn't handle it? I loved that woman, man. I loved you! Every time I see you on TV, she starts going on and on about, "Oh, look at Lester." All y'all had to do was tell me.

LESTER. Aw, man.

SAL. And let me tell you something else. Bev didn't bust my knees up. Tell them who busted my knees, Kirk.

KIRK. Icebox.

SAL. Gregory "Icebox" Hunter busted my knees up on November 13th 1983. A Friday night game. I took a screen pass and he caught me at the knee from the blind side. I heard the bones crack before I felt the pain. I knew it was over that very second. Icebox ruined my dreams, not Bev. That woman was there for me, man. Fucking Lester playing God and shit.

KIRK. Yeah, but, Sal—

SAL. Don't yeah but Sal me. Suppose one of us told you Dee gave us the buzzard?

KIRK. Y'all would know about something I don't know about. Huckle my berry!

SAL. You damn right. Don't nobody want to be around hearing people say yeah, his woman got some good pussy. Is that what you say, Lester, when you see me and Bev?

LESTER. I don't think about that—

SAL. Why not? You talk about all the other women you ever had in your life. You talk about the one you with now. What category you put Bev in?

KIRK. You was listening the whole time.

SAL. You motherfucking right I was listening! I'm from Harlem, I hear every goddamn thing!

LESTER. OK, Sal, it was a long time ago, what the point in—

SAL. What's the point? What's the point? I'll show you what's the point.

(SAL attacks LESTER, punching him in the face. LESTER fights back but SAL is obviously getting the best of LESTER. KIRK and ALEX try to separate them. CHUCK retrieves the pistol from KIRK's bag. He fires it into the air. Everything stops.)

CHUCK. Stop it! Stop it! I swear to God in heaven I'll shoot everybody! I said stop it!

LESTER. We stopped!

KIRK. Give me the gun, Chuck.

CHUCK. No.

ALEX. Chuck—

CHUCK. Shut up! Do any of you know what I have been through. You wanna know how much I agonized about coming here. Insulting me, ignoring me. *(He shoots the gun. Everyone is quiet and still.)* Like it don't matter. Where's the love I was supposed to find? No matter how hard I try, I can't give up my past. And my past is you fucking assholes!

(The WOMEN enter.)

FREIDA. Alex!

BEV. What happened?

CHUCK. Don't say anything to me. Because nothing matters. Right, Dee?

DIANE. No, Chuck.

CHUCK. Only God, right, Dee? Where is God now!?

DIANE. Right here, Chuck.

CHUCK. That's some funny shit, Dee. God does have a sense of humor.

BEV. Chuck—

CHUCK. What?

BEV. You don't want to kill anybody.

CHUCK. Yes, I do! Because it's the Fourth of July. A nothing matters kinda holiday, right, Alex?

(KIRK approaches CHUCK. CHUCK fires the gun over KIRK's head. KIRK runs for cover.)

KIRK. Shoot at me and call me bunny rabbit! Damn, Chuck! This is me—Kirk!

DIANE. Chuck, we are your family. We love you.

CHUCK. Why? Because I got the gun?

BEV. Chuck, look at everybody. We have come a long way. Why don't you put the gun down.

CHUCK. I am tired! Tired! First I got to try and be somebody I'm not because the world says you can't be this way, you have to be that way. So I turn to God for answers. I tell the congregation that I am gay, they tell me I am a sinner. God doesn't love you. You are going to burn in hell. Nobody told me my hell would be here on earth. I haven't even seen my daughters in six years! Did any of you know that? Liz told the judge, "They got a degenerate liar for a father." Did any of you know that? If you think the world gives a black man a hard time— I

can deal with the world but y'all supposed to know me.
I feel so lonely and lost sometimes.

LESTER. Chuck, I'm sorry, man.

CHUCK (*points the gun at LESTER*). Don't apologize to
me! Apologize to Sal and Bev!

LESTER. Sorry.

CHUCK. Mean it! Say I'm sorry for being a self-centered
asshole.

LESTER. I'm sorry for being such a self-centered asshole,
Sal.

DIANE. Chuck, think about how y'all used to be. Do that
for me please. I used to watch y'all walking across the
145th Street bridge. Young, proud, black, confident, like
warriors, like you could conquer the world.

CHUCK. But look at us now.

KIRK. That was us, Chuck.

CHUCK. What does it matter, Lieutenant Bright!

DIANE. It matters, Chuck, you know that.

LESTER. Remember how my father used to pull us right
off the street, throw us in the car and take us to Coney
Island to ride the Cyclone, or to Shea to see the Mets.

KIRK. Sal's dad usta trap us in the room and read passages
of the Bible to us. "Neither do men put new wine into
old bottles: else the bottles break, and the wine runneth
out, and the bottles perish; but they put new wine into
new bottles, and both are preserved." Matthew, chapter 9,
verse 17.

CHUCK. It doesn't matter!

KIRK. Only verse I know by heart.

ALEX. Remember when Lester tried to be a gangster and
starting hanging out with Alimo on 138th Street doing
holdups?

LESTER. Sometimes all that feels so far away and sometimes it feels like yesterday.

ALEX. You lucky, Lester, they almost pinned that Central Park murder on you.

LESTER. They was going to let me take the fall for that, if Chuck and Sal didn't put the fear of God in Alimo.

KIRK. Sal, what did you say to Alimo, of all people, that got Lester off.

SAL. It wasn't me. It was Chuck. I got a .38 from Scottie. Me and Chuck walked up to 139th Street and found Alimo selling dope in the hallway. I put the gun to his head and Chuck told him he had to get Lester out of the situation he was in. He told him he didn't care if it was him, or his whole crew, but they was going to have to get Lester off. Everybody knew Lester didn't kill nobody. But the cops would see just another black face. That's all they wanted was a face. I cocked the gun at Alimo's head and Chuck told him, "Not now but right now." Alimo turned one of his flunkies in. He knew we was serious as cancer because the chances of us getting caught—one black kid killing another—was slim to nothing. He stood a better chance dealing with the police.

(LESTER begins to weep. CHUCK is almost in a trance, still holding the gun.)

DIANE. Remember that, Chuck?

SAL. Fuck Chuck! You wanna kill me, go ahead. You ain't contact nobody for years. Look, man, I don't understand none of that gay shit but what's that got to do with anything? That ain't what's got me. I don't give a damn if you a faggot.

(CHUCK cocks the gun, points at SAL with intention.)

What's got me is that you kept that shit a secret all these years. What's wrong with me? You got a secret, my wife got secrets, Lester's got a secret. I ain't y'all's friend? I don't count? When Julius died, Lester sent flowers. Fuck flowers! Alex, you should have had your ass up in New York in a Al Sharpton minute protesting how they shot my boy down like a dog in the street because they thought he had a gun. And where were you, Chuck? Someplace being scared? We was all scared. That's why we formed the Bow-Wow Club. I'm still scared. I'm a black man in America, goddammit, hell yeah I'm scared. That's why this shit hurts so much. You want to ease my pain, shoot me. Go ahead. Shoot!

(SAL approaches CHUCK daring him to shoot. CHUCK tries to turn the gun to his mouth. SAL grabs the gun. They wrestle for a moment. SAL takes the gun. Then he hugs CHUCK who is weeping. He rocks him. A long moment of silence. Everybody is in shock.)

ALEX. Damn. I read a report a little while ago that said the life expectancy of a black man in Harlem is twenty-seven. I guess everybody here beat that statistic.

KIRK. I can run off a list of names as long as the A-train line of people who ain't here anymore.

LESTER. Nathaniel "Pop" Brown, shot dead.

SAL. My man, Rueben Figoroa.

ALEX. Charlie Bronson put a shotgun in his mouth and blew his head off.

KIRK. Cisco, they burned Hollis like a fried chicken—

LESTER. Gary Smith, Gary Green, Gary Jones, cut Mike Horry's lips off.

ALEX. Mousey, od'd, little Steve, Rennard, Killer—

LESTER. Rodney and Bryce—

KIRK. Rodney and Bryce.

SAL. Dwain and Darren—

ALEX. We been through a war and never knew we were in one. They keep killing us and we keep killing each other. *(Long pause.)*

FREIDA *(holding her stomach)*. Julius Anderson—

(There is a long silence. The name hangs in the air. BEV screams a piercing scream. SAL breaks down. He comforts his wife. Everyone is emotional. ALEX comforts FREIDA. LESTER hugs CHUCK. The hugs are exchanged among the group and are accompanied with "I'm sorrys," all except ALEX. LOITA holds LESTER. The last "I'm sorry" is from CHUCK to SAL.)

CHUCK. Sal, I'm sorry, I—

ALEX. Y'all about some sorry motherfuckers.

(CHUCK extends himself to ALEX.)

ALEX. Look. I apologize but I can do without the hug, all right? *(They shake hands.)* Chuck. Me and you got some talking to do.

CHUCK. I look forward to it, Alex. *(Another long silence.)*

DIANE. Lord! What are we going to do with our boys? If they don't want to thank you, I will thank you for them. Thank you, Jesus.

KIRK, LESTER, FREIDA & BEV. Amen.

DIANE. Y'all ready, because I ain't finish with you, mister. *(She starts walking off. KIRK follows her.)*

KIRK. Dee, hey, Dee, you want me to get on my knees? Dee, "Love has no desire but to fulfill itself—" *(They exit.)*

FREIDA *(her meaning is different from DIANE's)*. And I'm not finish with you, Professor Alex Earle. *(She walks off.)*

ALEX. Baby, look, baby— *(ALEX walks off. BEV starts to leave.)*

SAL. Bev?

BEV. What, Sal?

SAL. Nothing. *(They share a short moment and exit.)*

LESTER. Let's go, Chuck.

CHUCK. I'll be right there.

LOITA. Were you really going to shoot everybody?

CHUCK. I think I was.

LOITA. Wow.

(LESTER and LOITA exit. CHUCK surveys his surroundings. Suddenly the sound of howling wolves is heard. CHUCK listens, then he howls. The howl is joined by the others, including the WOMEN. They blend in with the wolves, with the night.)

CHUCK. The Bow-Wow Club! Ruff-ruff. The Bow-Wow Club! Ruff-ruff. *(He exits chanting.)*

THE END

PRODUCTION NOTES

SETTING

Act One

The modest new home of Kirk and Diane Bright. Visible should be a kitchen, dining room, living room and guest room. There is a door in the kitchen which leads to a backyard area. The sunken living room is equipped with a convertible sofa, end tables, stereo and bar. There should be an archway entrance to the living room. Beyond the arch, a hall leading to the bedrooms (not visible).

Act Two

A park in Maryland. There should be two large picnic tables and a tree or tree stump. One should get the feeling that you are deep in the woods.

A NOTE ABOUT THE SONGS

All songs used throughout the script are the author's own. Producing companies are encouraged to put their own melody to the lyrics of these few songs.

ADDITIONAL CHARACTER NOTES

DIANE BRIGHT: Housewife and mother of three, and loves it. Born again. A large woman.

KIRK BRIGHT: He and Diane have been married for 16 years. They own a brand new home. He is gregarious and jovial, laughs a lot. May be a little overweight.

SAL ANDERSON: Former star football prospect. Married to Beverly for 15 years. Angry and bitter. Possibly an alcoholic. Walks with a limp.

BEVERLY ANDERSON: About to take the bar exam for the first time. Wants out of her marriage.

ALEXANDER EARLE: A college professor of African-American history. Serious, but not taken seriously by the Bow-Wow Club. Recently married to Frieda.

FREIDA EARLE: White. Politically and culturally aware.

CHUCK HOOTER: Associate professor of philosophy and religion. Former minister. Soft-spoken but intense.

LESTER MCMICHAEL: World renown singer and dancer. A confirmed ladies' man who has lived a charmed life. Extremely sharp dresser.

LOITA CLARVEAX: Lester's latest girlfriend. Sexy and exotic, 5 ft. 9 in. or taller. Has her own way of looking at the world.

PERRY PENNICK: Preppy and realistic. Doesn't know when to stop talking.

DIRECTOR'S NOTES

DIRECTOR'S NOTES

DIRECTOR'S NOTES

DIRECTOR'S NOTES

DIRECTOR'S NOTES